BUILDING WEALTH
& loving it

A down-to-earth guide to
personal finance & investing

JIMMY B. PRINCE

Wrightbooks

First published 2010 by Wrightbooks
an imprint of John Wiley & Sons Australia, Ltd
42 McDougall Street, Milton Qld 4064

Office also in Melbourne

Typeset in Adobe Garamond 12.5/15.5pt

© Jimmy B Prince 2010

The moral rights of the author have been asserted

National Library of Australia Cataloguing-in-Publication data:

Author:	Prince, Jimmy B.
Title:	Building wealth and loving it: a down-to-earth guide to personal finance & investing / Jimmy B Prince.
ISBN:	9781742169958 (pbk.)
Notes:	Includes index.
Subjects:	Finance, Personal. Wealth. Investments. Cash management.
Dewey Number:	332.024

Cover image © danzo80, 2009, used under license from Shutterstock.com

Tables on pages 51, 234 and 241: Australian Taxation Office <www.ato.gov.au> 2008, copyright commonwealth of Australia, reproduced by permission.

Printed in China by Printplus Limited

10 9 8 7 6 5 4 3 2 1

Disclaimer
The material in this publication is of the nature of general comment only, and does not represent professional advice. It is not intended to provide specific guidance for particular circumstances and it should not be relied on as the basis for any decision to take action or not take action on any matter which it covers. Readers should obtain professional advice where appropriate, before making any such decision. To the maximum extent permitted by law, the author and publisher disclaim all responsibility and liability to any person, arising directly or indirectly from any person taking or not taking action based upon the information in this publication.

Contents

About the author

Jim Prince is a fellow of CPA Australia and a tax specialist. He is a former lecturer and tutor in income tax law at La Trobe University, and teaches a number of wealth creation courses for the CAE in Melbourne. He has authored several investment books including *Tax for Australians For Dummies* and has written articles for *Your Mortgage* magazine and <http://thebull.com. au>. In 2000 Jim was nominated for an Adult Learners Week 2000 outstanding tutor award.

In his earlier years Jim worked for the Australian Taxation Office and also consulted to CPA Australia 'Technicall'.

Preface

Many years ago I regularly bought lotto tickets on the off-chance that I would become an instant millionaire. For a small outlay of a few dollars I would select six numbers and hope they'd be the ones that'd be drawn out of the barrel. On one occasion, while I was watching the draw on television, I happened to get the first number. And within a matter of seconds I had the second one. When I got the third number I became a little excited. When the fourth number came out I called my wife, as this was starting to get a little serious. When the fifth consecutive number was drawn I was within seconds of becoming an instant millionaire. While I was waiting for the last number to appear, a voice from the beyond casually whispered the following message in my ear, 'Ah, sorry mate, you're not meant to win'. And what normally happens when you get such a message? I missed the last number by the narrowest of margins. If I had selected 26 rather than 27 I would have been an instant millionaire. When I recovered from the shock of missing out on the chance of a lifetime, I concluded if the lotto gods weren't going to make me wealthy, I'll need to turn to plan B and try to do it myself.

There are many ways to build up your wealth. They can range from saving and trying to do it quickly at the casino or races to the thrill and fun of building wealth from investing in shares and property. While sitting in the comfort of your chair or resting by the pool sipping a cold drink, it's possible to literally make heaps if the value of your investments — especially your share portfolio — were to rise. But you can also lose it just as quickly. The secret to wealth creation is a willingness to have a fair-dinkum go, and not to overemphasise the risks. Sure you can lose money along the way — but let's be positive here, you can also make a truckload as well.

Building wealth is similar to driving a car. When you sit behind the steering wheel there's a risk you could have an accident, and cars are costly to keep on the road. But the rewards you will gain from driving will encourage you to keep plugging along. When you invest you'll need to know what you're doing. And that will come from understanding the basics and getting good advice from the professionals. Potential investors often come to me and say, 'I'm eager to invest *but* I'm scared of losing money'. Welcome to the club. You're not the only one. Concerns that you could lose money are natural feelings you're likely to experience. Unfortunately, when you invest there's no-one out there ringing the bell to tell you whether you're on a sure winner. If it was that easy we would all be winners. I always say to potential investors, 'If you're afraid to have a go, what are the alternatives?' The answer is quite simple: put your money in a term deposit and lose it that way. Because if you persist with this strategy (although your money may be safe), your wealth is not going to grow. Regrettably, there is no cast-iron guarantee that whatever decision you make is going to be the best option. Over the years I've lost heaps and made my fair share of mistakes. But I've also made some great investment decisions. So if you do happen to make the odd mistake along the way try not to dwell on it—what's done is done. Sitting in the corner and feeling sorry for yourself or vowing never to invest again is not going to solve the problem. The solution is quite simple: see where you went wrong and move on.

This book will appeal to readers who would prefer to read a one-stop book that will conveniently cover all the major ways of investing to build wealth. It's written in plain English and explains in simple terms the core investment principles and tax issues you need to be aware of. This book is written in three parts, all centred on the general theme of building wealth:

$ part I: let the games begin: getting organised

$ part II: watch your money grow: building wealth

$ part III: reaping the harvest: superannuation and retirement.

Throughout the book you will find numerous practical case studies and handy tips to help you understand core investment principles and to reinforce the learning process. So let the games begin. It's time to build wealth and love it. Incidentally, if you make $100 000 after you read this book, you owe me lunch!

Jim Prince
Melbourne
December 2009

Part I

Let the games begin: getting organised

There are many reasons for wanting to build wealth, ranging from a desire for security to wanting to make a heap of cash. All are valid reasons if you can manage it. But before you can kick-start the process you've got to lay down the foundations, including preparing a budget and planning ahead. If you can get this right at the outset you'll be well on the way to building wealth and loving it. In part I we examine how to prepare a budget and the key steps you'll need to examine before you start investing. This part also covers choosing a suitable investment structure and issues associated with borrowing money to help you to build up your wealth.

Chapter 1

Laying down the foundations

The first question I ask participants who attend my wealth creation courses is why they need to build wealth. The answers normally range from gaining security and freedom to a strong desire to make lots of money. All noteworthy answers if you can pull it off! To achieve these objectives you'll need to do some boring stuff like preparing a budget and planning ahead. In this chapter I chat about the key things you'll need to do before you can kick-start your wealth-creation adventures.

Your capacity to build wealth is primarily dependent on the amount of net disposable income you earn. Net disposable income is income you've got available after you pay income tax. And of course the more income you can generate the greater the opportunity to build up your wealth.

As is the case if you plan to erect a dwelling, before you can start accumulating wealth you've got to lay down the foundations. So here are some of the things you should consider doing first:

$ prepare a budget

$ list your assets and liabilities

$ set your goals

$ be prepared.

Prepare a budget

The first thing on the agenda is to prepare a budget. This is a simple financial plan that will allow you to keep track of all your expenses and income. So whenever you open your wallet or purse or get a bill (for instance, telephone, gas or electricity), jot down the details on a spreadsheet over a given period of time (for instance, 12 months). An example of how you might format this is given in table 1.1, on page 6. When you do this you'll start to find out stuff like:

$ your spending habits

$ the different types of expenses you incur

$ the amount you spend each week

$ the dates when bills become due for payment

$ your ability to pay bills on time

$ what bills you'll incur in the future

$ what to cut back if you get into financial difficulty.

Next you should record all your cash inflows (as illustrated in table 1.2, on page 7)—for example, your net salary and wages and any investment income you derive (such as dividends, interest and rent)—plus the dates you expect to receive them. You'll generally find these cash inflows will tend to be fixed and regular. You should also record any one-off payments you're likely to receive (for example, a tax refund). It will then become a simple exercise of comparing your cash inflows with your cash outflows (see table 1.2, on page 7).

Having this valuable information on hand will give you some degree of certainty and control over your financial affairs. It'll provide you with information like the amount you can save over a given period and how much you can afford to borrow. A budget will also help you plan ahead to cover potential shortfalls (deficits) you may occur in the future, and what to do with any surpluses you may accumulate.

Handy tip

If you want some more information about how to prepare a personal budget, visit Wikipedia's personal budget site at ‹http://en.wikipedia.org/wiki/Personal_budget›.

List your assets and liabilities

After you've got your budget up and running, the next thing on your 'to do' list is a stocktake of all your assets and liabilities. This will help you keep track of what you own and owe and can come in handy if you're looking for a loan (see chapter 4). It will also give you confidence that you're in total control of your financial affairs. Make sure you keep your records in an orderly manner: you'll need to access these documents when preparing your individual tax return (otherwise your accountant is likely to charge you heaps trying to fix up the mess). Your accountant and/or a financial planner can help you with this exercise.

Table 1.1: cash outflows

Date	Amount	Monthly total	Internet	Phone	Electric	Gas	Water	Car rego	Insurance	House loan	Rates	Medical	Food	Spending	Credit Card
05-Jan-00	$273			$273											
14-Jan-00	$660		$60										$600		
29-Jan-00	$396				$396										
30-Jan-00	$1704									$560		$223	$600	$100	$221
		$3033													
05-Feb-00	$101					$101									
11-Feb-00	$581			$181							$400				
14-Feb-00	$60		$60												
14-Feb-00	$600												$600		
20-Feb-00	$160						$160								
28-Feb-00	$1609									$560		$223	$600	$100	$126
		$3111													
05-Mar-00	$849			$207				$642							
14-Mar-00	$660		$60										$600		
31-Mar-00	$1824									$560		$223	$600	$100	$341
		$3333													

Table 1.2: cash inflows

	Jan	Feb	Mar	Apr	May	June	July	Aug	Sept	Oct	Nov	Dec	Total
Net salary and wages	$3916	$3916	$3916	$3916	$3916	$3916	$3964	$3964	$3964	$3964	$3964	$3964	$47 280
Interest			$56			$62			$65			$68	$251
Dividends				$1250						$1456			$2706
Rent													
Tax refund								$1347					$1347
Total cash inflow	**$3916**	**$3916**	**$3972**	**$5166**	**$3916**	**$3978**	**$3964**	**$5311**	**$4029**	**$5420**	**$3964**	**$4032**	**$51 584**
Less													
Total cash outflow	$3033	$3111	$3333	$3322	$7072	$3902	$4416	$3974	$2899	$2809	$3274	$4893	$46 038
Surplus	$883	$805	$639	$1844		$76		$1337	$1130	$2611	$690		$5546
Shortfall					-$3156		-$452					-$861	
Net cash inflow/ outflow	**$883**	**$805**	**$639**	**$1844**	**-$3156**	**$76**	**-$452**	**$1337**	**$1130**	**$2611**	**$690**	**-$861**	**$5546**

Record your assets

Your assets can range from your favourite frypan, furniture and personal belongings to your most prized Rolls Royce, shares and property. With respect to wealth-creating assets like shares and real estate, keep proper records and constantly monitor whether they're making money for you. While doing this exercise keep in mind, 'the first rule to building wealth is not to lose it!' These are some of the things you'll need to record:

$ *Shares.* Next to each company jot down the date you bought them and the purchase price. You can get this information from the buy contract notes you receive from your stockbroker (see chapter 8). You can quickly calculate how your share portfolio is performing by simply comparing the purchase price with its current market price. Online stockbrokers have watch lists that can automatically do this for you. You should also record any dividend payments you're likely to receive in your budget statement (see table 1.2).

$ *Property.* Record the date you bought any property you own and the purchase price. You can get this information from the contract of sale. Also keep track of any improvements you make to your properties and the dates you do them. You'll need this information to calculate whether you've made a capital gain or capital loss for tax purposes (see chapter 13). A ballpark way of assessing whether a property is a good investment is checking how long it takes to double in value. Ideally you would like to see this happen every seven to 10 years. I chat about this in more detail in chapter 12.

$ *Term deposits.* Keep details of the amount you've invested, the maturity date and rate of interest you've locked into.

You should also record the amount of interest you receive in your budget statement (see table 1.2). I discuss investing in fixed-interest securities in more detail in chapter 5.

$ *Managed funds.* Keep the regular statements your managed fund sends you and check the opening and closing balances. This will tell you whether you're making money or losing money. The rate of any potential growth will depend on the investment strategy you've selected (which can range from capital stable to growth), and the fees you'll incur to manage your money. I chat about managed funds in chapter 6.

$ *Superannuation fund.* Super funds are required to issue regular 'benefit statements' setting out the opening and closing balance at a particular date (usually on 30 June). As super funds are managed funds, any potential growth will depend on the investment strategy you're relying on to grow your money (which can range from capital stable to growth) and the fees you're paying. By the way, it's possible to check online how your super fund's performing on a daily basis: the superannuation fund you belong to can show you how to do this. I chat about superannuation in chapters 15 and 16.

$ *Your prized collectables.* They can range from your jewellery, stamp or coin collections to antiques and paintings. Keep detailed records, especially for items that cost more than $500, as you're liable to pay capital gains tax if you make a capital gain on sale. I chat about collectables in chapter 2.

Handy tip

As cars depreciate with age you're technically losing money from the moment you buy one, unless it's a much-sought-after vintage or classic that car buffs are willing to pay heaps to own.

Keep track of your liabilities

To meet all your legal obligations you should list, combine and prioritise all your financial commitments. Liabilities are normally listed in the order they're due for repayment. Payments due within a short period (for instance, one month) are called current liabilities. They can range from your household bills (such as gas, electricity and telephone) to ongoing credit card, mortgage and loan repayments. On the other hand, payments not due within 12 months are called long-term liabilities. Incidentally, as credit cards normally charge you a high rate of interest on cash advances, try to pay these loans off as quickly as possible. Also take full advantage of any interest-free period on purchases (for instance, up to 55 days) that your credit cards may offer you.

> **Handy tip**
>
> Under Australian tax law you can set up a Capital Gains Tax (CGT) asset register to help you keep track of all your CGT assets (rather than keep a pile of documents). If you want to record your CGT assets in this register, the information must be certified by a registered tax agent or a person approved by the Tax Office. For more details read the Australian Taxation Office publication *Guide to capital gains tax* (NAT 4151) and particularly the section titled 'Keeping Records — Asset registers'. You can download a copy from the Tax Office website ‹www.ato.gov.au›.

Set your goals

Setting goals are your blueprints to building wealth (for instance, to derive income and capital growth). It pays to have clearly defined objectives in mind to inspire you to do something. To get the ball rolling, consider writing down what you wish to accomplish within a certain time frame. The tricky bit is the nuts and bolts you'll need to put into place to achieve these goals.

For example, one core objective could be to accumulate sufficient capital to fund your retirement. To do this you'll need to know the amount you'll have to accumulate; how long it will take; and how you intend to get there. A qualified financial planner can help you with this exercise. For instance, one option could be to make regular contributions to your superannuation fund. You might consider 60 per cent of your final average salary a reasonable sum to fund your lifestyle in retirement. The capital you'll need to accumulate is generally 15 times your desired pension. So if you're seeking a $50 000 pension, according to the formula you'll need to have at least $750 000 in your war chest. Once you've set your goal—a $50 000 pension—it becomes a question of what you'll need to set aside each week, and choosing an appropriate investment strategy that'll help you get there. Superannuation funds normally provide calculators on their respective websites to help you do this calculation (for instance, check out HESTA <www.hesta.com.au> and Westpac-ASFA Retirement Standard <www.superannuation.asn.au/RS/default.aspx>).

When you set your goals make sure they're realistic and achievable. Setting a goal to make $10 million in five years may sound like a great idea. But trying to do it within certain financial constraints (for instance, you only earn $60 000 per annum) can quickly bring you back to reality. To kick-start the process it pays to set achievable targets first (for example, save a specific amount within a given period), then raise the bar and start again.

Be prepared

There is an old Boy Scout motto that you should try to keep in mind and that is 'be prepared'. And to this we can also add 'you've got to be in it to win'. In your endeavour to build wealth you should constantly be on the lookout for any good investment opportunities that could pop up unexpectedly. To ensure you're first in line it's important that you're able to access cash at short notice. It's no use saying, 'Well, I would have bought it if I had the money'. That may be so. But if you want to build wealth you have to plan ahead so that you'll not be put into this unfortunate situation. Remember opportunities can often only knock once.

There are many ways you can do this. For example, establish a line of credit that can remain dormant until you need to access those funds and/or take out a personal loan (see chapter 4). Another way of raising funds quickly is to sell shares you own. In chapter 7 I emphasise it normally takes no more than a few seconds to sell them and you'll normally get your money back within four days. Incidentally, one way of killing two birds with one stone is to sell your duds—those shares that are losing you money. If you do this it will give you an opportunity to recoup your losses by getting into something better. And to add icing to the cake, you'll crystallise a 'valuable tax loss' that you can deduct from a capital gain you make in the future (see chapter 9 and the case study at the end of this chapter).

The insurance policies you had to have

In the course of building up your wealth there's a risk you could suffer a financial loss. There are many different types of insurance policies you can take out to protect your assets, income and personal health. The main ones are:

⇒ property insurance to cover loss or damage to your property

⇒ house and contents insurance to protect your personal belongings

⇒ car insurance to cover theft or damage to your car

⇒ income protection insurance to cover loss of income

⇒ rent insurance to cover loss of rental receipts if you own a rental property

---

⇒   life insurance to provide benefits in the event of death

⇒   personal accident and illness insurance to cover trauma, injury and sickness

⇒   health insurance to cover medical and hospital expenses.

If you want to know more about taking out insurance you can visit the Insurance Council of Australia website ‹www.insurancecouncil. com.au›. And to find insurance brokers where you live, check out the National Insurance Brokers Association ‹www.niba.com.au›.

Make it happen

Last but not least is your enthusiasm to have a go and try to make it happen. As they say in the classics, he who hesitates is lost. I always emphasise to participants who attend my wealth creation courses that wealth creation is not rocket science. You need to have confidence that you can do it and that will come from understanding the fundamentals (see chapter 2). This is especially so if you plan to invest in the sharemarket, where share prices fluctuate daily, or real estate, where you'll need a substantial sum to own a property outright. So it's essential that you develop a positive attitude and don't overemphasise the negatives. Speaking from personal experience, one of the worst feelings is to look back in five years' time and see all the missed opportunities that have slipped through your fingers. Along the way you'll most likely make the odd mistake—unfortunately we all make mistakes—but chances are you'll also make some great buys. If you do make a mistake, see what you did wrong and move on.

Getting help: financial planners

If you're a complete novice or you're totally overwhelmed and confused about investing, a financial planner can steer you in the right direction. Financial planners are licensed professionals who can help you prepare an appropriate investment plan to help you achieve your objectives. They can also explain the different asset classes that are currently on the market and help you choose to suit your age, risk profile and goals. In return they'll charge you a fee for their services. There are a number of ways you can be charged for the advice they give you (for example, one-off fee, hourly basis, commission-based). So you should check this out at the outset. Also, before you commit yourself to any particular financial planner you should ask them:

$ whether they are properly licensed

$ whether they will be providing you with independent advice

$ whether they are associated with any particular financial institution

$ whether they will get any commissions and benefits for putting you into certain financial products. If so, how are they calculated and why will they be recommending these products to you — are there alternative options to compare and contrast?

For more details visit the Australian Securities and Investment Commission (ASIC) website <www.fido.gov.au> and read 'Choosing your adviser'. If you want to contact a financial planner you can visit the Australian Securities Exchange website <www. asx.com.au> and read 'Find a financial planner'. You should also visit the ASIC website <www.fido.gov.au> and go to 'financial tips and safety checks' and read 'Financial Planners' Code of Ethics and Rules of Professional Conduct'.

Case study: be prepared for the unexpected

One afternoon while Richard was happily counting all the money he was making on the stock market, his wife casually dropped a bombshell into his cosy bunker. She informed him she needed a new car, as the old one was on the verge of going to the big car yard in the sky. His immediate response was a firm 'NO!' But his wife knew he had a weak spot. While Richard was watching his football team on television his wife raised the topic again, just as his side was on the verge of a meritorious victory — and in a brief moment of insanity he said 'yes'. Before Richard could change his mind, his wife raced off to talk turkey with a number of car dealers she had discreetly lined up. The next day she informed him she had just bought the car she always wanted, and presented him with the bad news: a $30 000 bill!

When Richard recovered from the shock of having to part with such a large sum, he set himself the task of funding the transaction. As the new car would be ready in two weeks' time, he had some time up his sleeve. Richard's plan of attack would be to sell some shares. As shares can be sold in a matter of seconds, he knew he could get the necessary funds by the due date (see chapter 8). His main concern was which companies to sell. There's an old investment adage that you should 'cut your losses and let your winners run'. Richard could either sell his non-profitable companies and take a capital loss, or sell those companies that were making him money. If he sold the good stuff he could miss out on the possibility of making more money and would be liable to pay capital gains tax (yuck). As Richard had a few duds in his share portfolio he decided to take a capital loss. This is because he will gain two significant benefits: he will get rid of the dead wood and incur a capital loss that he can deduct from a current or future capital gain. By doing this he'll effectively save having to pay tax on any capital gain he makes (see chapter 9).

As Richard had a principle that you should avoid reducing your capital base, he decided to take out an interest-only loan and replace the duds he sold with quality blue chips that hopefully

Case study *(cont'd)*: be prepared for the unexpected

will recoup the money he lost (see chapter 4). By doing this he'll be buying an investment that will derive income, and the interest is a tax-deductible expense! On the other hand, if Richard had borrowed the money to buy the car outright, the interest would not have been tax deductible as the car is for private use. Richard will use the dividends he'll derive to help meet the interest repayments, and his cash flow will not be greatly affected (see chapter 4). To add icing to the cake Richard will be buying a quality investment that has the capacity to deliver capital growth. He's hoping this strategy would counter the fact that cars depreciate in value the moment you drive them out of the car yard. He also knew he had the option to quickly sell the shares and discharge the loan if necessary. In the meantime, if the shares increase in value — depending on how much they rise — Richard can sell a portion to repay the loan in full!

There is, of course, an element of risk that Richard could lose money if the cards don't fall his way. But as they say in the classics, nothing ventured, nothing gained. I chat about risk in more detail in chapter 2.

Chapter 2

Building wealth the smart way

How often do you hear of potential investors moaning over lost opportunities: 'If I had purchased those shares (or that particular property) five years ago I would've made a fortune.' Right? Well, in hindsight we're all wise after the event. Unfortunately, there's no-one out there ringing the bell telling you when it's the best time to buy or sell your investments. If it was that easy we would all be rolling in dough. In this chapter I explain the basic steps of what to do to become a successful investor. I also compare the two dominant investments you're likely to consider: shares versus real estate.

Before you open your wallet or purse and start investing it pays to follow the five basic steps that I chat about in this chapter. This is of particular importance if you're planning to invest a substantial amount in a complex investment structure that only a financial genius could understand. These steps are:

1   understand the fundamentals

2   identify the benefits

3   check out the risks

4   examine the tax issues

5   make sense of economic data.

Step 1: understand the fundamentals

A friend who was keen to start a share portfolio and make money in a bull market (where share prices are continually rising) contacted me and said, 'I need some urgent advice about investing in shares. Could you quickly tell me what I need to do?' When I get these types of questions I always remember what the American showman PT Barnum said many years ago: 'There's a sucker born every minute'.

Investments can include putting money into:

$ traditional investments (such as fixed interest, shares and real estate)

$ managed funds (and managed investment schemes) managed by Australia's leading financial institutions

$ collectables (such as wine, antiques, vintage cars and works of art).

When putting together a suitable investment portfolio there are many factors you'll need to compare and contrast. Each asset class will have specific features that may or may not appeal to you (see table 2.1). The tricky bit is trying to understand what you're doing and how to separate the wheat from the chaff. For example, if you like shares because they tick all the right boxes (for instance, provides income, capital growth, tax benefits, liquidity, minimal entry and exit fees, and no holding costs), the trade-off is 'volatility', meaning there's a risk they can fall in value. On the other hand, if you would prefer the safety features that a fixed-interest investment can offer you, the trade-off here is no capital growth. The ideal investment mix will depend on your age, risk profile and your personal preference to investing. There's an old saying that goes along the lines, 'if investments are keeping you awake at night—sell down to the sleeping point'. If you find this a little overwhelming you can always seek professional advice from a qualified financial planner (see chapter 1).

Table 2.1: asset classes at a glance

Benefits	Fixed interest	Shares	Real estate	Managed funds	Collectables
Income	Yes	Yes	Yes	Yes	No
Capital growth	No	Yes	Yes	Yes	Yes
Tax benefits	No	Yes	Yes	Yes	Yes
Volatility	Low	High	Medium	Medium	Low
Liquidity	High	High	Low	High	Low
Entry fees	No	Minimal	High	Minimal	High
Exit fees	No	Minimal	High	Minimal	High
Holding costs	No	No	Yes	Yes	Optional

Fixed interest

When you invest in interest-bearing securities (for example, term deposits), you'll be depositing your money with reputable financial institutions, such as banks and building societies, that are regulated by federal laws. In return you'll receive a fixed rate of interest (for example, 6 per cent per annum), and when the loan matures you would expect to get your initial capital back. By the way, during the 2008–09 global financial crisis, deposits up to a specified amount were government-guaranteed. This investment is worth considering if you're seeking security, especially if you see alternate investments like shares and real estate valuations falling by the wayside. I chat about the pros and cons of investing in interest-bearing securities in chapter 5.

Shares

When you buy shares that are listed on the Australian Securities Exchange (ASX) you will become a part-owner of major Australian companies such as BHP Billiton, Telstra and Woolworths. And you'll be predominantly relying on these companies running profitable businesses for steady income and capital growth. As a rule of thumb, the more profitable they become the more money you're likely to make. So if you want to start a quality share portfolio you should find out what these companies do to generate revenue. You should also check out the key performance indicators to see whether they're trading profitably. I chat about the sharemarket in more detail in chapters 7 to 11.

Investment mix: shares and stable fixed interest

There is a school of thought regarding the ideal mix between shares and fixed interest. To work out how much you should put into the sharemarket simply subtract your age from 100. For example, if you're 20 years of age 80 per cent should be in the sharemarket and 20 per cent in stable fixed interest. On the other hand, if you're 60 years of age, invest 40 per cent in the sharemarket and 60 per cent in stable fixed interest.

Real estate

If your plan is to invest in real estate you'll be basically investing in bricks and mortar (land and buildings) for steady income and capital growth. There's an old adage that when it comes to real estate there are only three things you need to consider: location, location and location. As a general rule the better the location the more you stand to make. I examine investing in real estate in more detail in chapters 12 to 14.

Managed funds

Managed funds and managed investment schemes are mutual investment funds managed by Australia's leading financial institutions. They give small investors the opportunity to invest in a wide variety of domestic and foreign investment options. This could be a great way of investing if you're an inexperienced investor or you would prefer someone to manage your money for you. I chat about the pros and cons of this way of investing in chapter 6. Incidentally, when you make a contribution to a complying superannuation fund you are effectively putting money into a managed fund (unless you run a self managed super fund). I chat about superannuation funds in chapters 15 and 16.

Collectables

Collectables can range from collecting bottle tops, footy cards and butterflies to stamps, wine and paintings. If you're a serious collector you'll be hoping they'll increase in value and make heaps of money for you. Unfortunately, while you're waiting to find out, it's unlikely you'll derive income and you could incur ongoing holding costs (for instance, insurance and security expenses). To add salt to the wound there's no guarantee you'll make a capital gain on sale. So if you want to invest in collectables you should check out the following:

$ *What's collectable.* The first thing to do is find out what type of collectables could increase in value (for instance, a rare stamp or painting by a famous artist).

$ *Market value.* Make sure you don't pay more than it's worth. Examining catalogues, attending auctions and seeking professional advice can help you here.

$ *Supply and demand.* Generally the rarer the item the greater the chance you'll make a capital gain down the track, as other collectors will be keen to buy it from you.

$ *Condition.* There are many variables you'll need to examine. For example, a slight tear or chip will affect a particular item's freshness and appeal. A slight error of judgement here could cost you dearly.

$ *Established market.* Make sure there's an established market where you can go and sell your collectables. Fortunately, there are many auction houses that deal with popular collectables such as paintings, antiques, stamps and coins that you can visit.

Handy tip

Keep an eye out for rare or unique items such as a much-sought-after vintage car and items associated with a famous historical person or sporting personality (make sure you get a certificate of authenticity to prove this is the case). Although these types of collectables can appreciate in value they could cost many thousands of dollars plus a hefty buyer's commission to get one. For example, a cricket bat owned by Sir Donald Bradman was recently sold for $145 000.

Under Australian tax law collectables are defined as artwork, jewellery, an antique, a coin or medallion, a rare folio, manuscript or book, a postage stamp or first day cover that is used or kept mainly for your personal use and enjoyment. Unfortunately, if any of these types of collectables cost more than $500, you could be liable to pay capital gains tax (CGT) if you make a capital gain on sale. One notable exception is cars. So if you like collecting vintage and classic cars (or collectables that cost $500 or less), you'll be laughing all the way to the bank if you make a capital gain on sale, as no tax is payable (see figure 2.1).

Figure 2.1: collectables

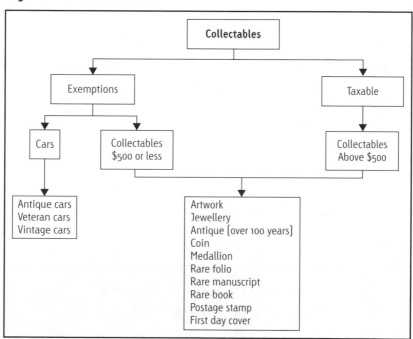

Step 2: identify the benefits

The next thing you should do is list all the benefits (and advantages) that a particular investment could offer you. This exercise will help you to compare and contrast the various benefits you can gain from holding specific investments. It will also tell you the trade-offs you'll need to make to get them.

Fixed interest

Benefits:

$ *Income.* Interest is normally credited to your account on a monthly, quarterly, half-yearly or yearly basis.

$ *Liquidity.* When the loan matures you will immediately get back the amount you initially invested.

$ *No entry and exit fees.* There are no entry and exit fees to worry about, although you could incur a penalty if you terminate your loan before the maturity date.

$ *No holding costs.* There are no ongoing costs associated with deriving interest.

Trade-off:

$ *No capital growth* (although you can invest in 'inflation-linked bonds' — see chapter 5).

$ *No tax benefits.*

Shares

Benefits:

$ *Income.* Companies normally pay two dividends each year — an interim or mid-year dividend and a final or end-of-year dividend.

$ *Capital growth.* Shares have the capacity to increase in value. You'll generally find capital growth is primarily dependent on a company's ability to grow its business and make more profits.

$ *Tax benefits.* If you borrow money to buy shares in companies that pay dividends the interest payments are tax deductible. And if your shares pay franked dividends you'll receive a franking credit tax offset (see chapter 9).

$ *Liquidity.* As shares can be sold within a matter of seconds they are said to be very liquid, which is a significant benefit to have up your sleeve if you need cash urgently.

$ *Prices published daily.* It's possible to make a quick profit if you see the price of your shares rise.

$ *Low entry and exit fees.* The costs of buying and selling shares are minimal.

$ *No holding costs.* There are no ongoing costs associated with owning shares.

Trade-off:

$ *Lose money.* The value of your shares could fall.

Real estate

Benefits:

$ *Income.* Rental properties normally pay income on a monthly basis.

$ *Capital growth.* Real estate has the capacity to increase in value. You'll generally find properties in good locations tend to double in value every seven to 10 years.

$ *Tax benefits.* Expenditure such as interest, rates, insurance, repairs and depreciation are tax deductible. You could also qualify for a capital works deduction (see chapter 13).

$ *Collateral.* Property can be offered as collateral to secure funds to buy wealth-creating assets like shares and real estate.

Trade-off:

$ *High barrier to entry.* It's a very expensive investment to get into.

$ *Liquidity.* It could take months to sell and the amount you'll receive depends on the price a willing buyer is prepared to pay.

$ *Entry and exit fees and holding costs.* There are high purchase and sale costs, and you'll incur ongoing costs which could be substantial.

$ *Lose money.* Property valuations could fall and your property could become vacant.

Managed funds

Benefits:

$ *Income.* Managed funds normally pay income twice a year.

$ *Capital growth.* Potential for capital growth if your investment units increase in value.

$ *Tax benefits.* If you have shares that pay franked dividends you'll receive a franking credit tax offset and tax-free distributions if you invest in property trusts (see chapter 6).

$ *Liquidity.* Your investment units can be sold quickly and you'll normally get your money back within seven days.

$ *Minimal entry and exit fees.* The cost of buying and selling your investment units are minimal.

Trade-off:

$ *Holding Costs.* You'll incur ongoing costs.

$ *Lose money.* Your investment units could fall in value.

Collectables

Benefits:

$ *Capital growth.* Certain collectables (for example, paintings) have the capacity to increase in value.

$ *Tax benefits.* Capital gains on collectables that cost $500 or less are disregarded. Also gains on certain collectables (for instance, vintage cars) are exempt from tax.

Trade-off:

$ *Entry and exit fees and holding costs.* There are high purchases and sale costs and you could incur ongoing costs (for example, insurance and security costs).

$ *Liquidity.* It could take months to sell and the amount you'll receive depends on the price a willing buyer is prepared to pay.

$ *Lose money.* Collectables could fall in value and you will derive no income.

$ *Capital losses.* Any capital loss you incur on sale of a collectable can only be deducted from any capital gain you make on sale of other collectables.

Step 3: check out the risks

When you invest in any of the asset classes mentioned here there's a risk they could decrease in value. Worse still, you could even lose the lot if it turns out to be a dud. There's also a risk the government could introduce certain policies that could have an adverse impact on your investment strategy (for instance, the amount you can put into super and when you can access those funds). Keep in mind the risk of losing your capital starts from the moment you hand your money over to someone to use or invest on your behalf. Unfortunately, if you want to build wealth, particularly your income and capital base, there are inherent risks that this may not occur. Some asset classes are more risky than others. For example, although shares and property can give you capital growth opportunities if valuations increase, the trade-off is you could lose money if they fall. To add salt to the wound your income flow could fall or cease if a company performs poorly or your property becomes vacant. On the other hand, if you decide to take the safe option and keep your money in a bank, your capital will not grow. Further, there's a risk the purchasing power of your capital will diminish because of inflation, and the return on your investment could fall if interest rates fall (see chapter 5). And if you decide it would be safer to keep your money under your mattress (as suggested by Malcolm Fraser during the 1983 election campaign!), there's a risk you could get robbed or your house could burn down. So when it comes to building wealth, unfortunately nothing is 100 per cent bulletproof!

Managing risk

Identifying your risk is one thing. Being able to cope with it is a separate issue. There are three key principles associated with managing risk that are worth considering.

Diversification

You've all heard the often-quoted investment adage that 'you should never put all your eggs in one basket' — or as they say in the classics, portfolio diversification makes up for investor ignorance.

To reduce the impact of risk it's prudent that you spread your risk and invest in different asset classes. For example:

$ term deposits with different maturity dates (see chapter 5)

$ managed funds that invest in a range of domestic and overseas investment options (see chapter 6)

$ shares in leading companies from different sectors of the Australian economy (see chapter 10). By the way, it's also possible for you to buy options to hedge (protect) your shares in a volatile market (see chapter 7)

$ residential property in specific suburbs (for instance, inner urban) and commercial property (see chapters 12 and 14). It's also possible to invest in property trusts that invest in different types of property such as residential accommodation, office space, industrial, rural and large shopping centres (see chapter 6).

Risk relative to return

There's another old investment adage that's worth keeping in mind and that is 'the higher the rate the higher the risk'. For example, you come across a property development that can potentially earn you up to 20 per cent per annum. Too good to be true? Well, you're probably right. I always like to apply the smell test, especially if investments like term deposits are paying around five per cent. You don't have to be Einstein to figure out the investment will have to make more than 20 per cent to pay you this rate plus a decent profit for the promoters. You'll generally find risk relative to return is quite high, and there's a strong possibility of failure if everything doesn't go according to plan. Before you sign anything you should seek advice from a qualified professional such as an accountant, solicitor or financial planner. I always say it's better to be safe than sorry.

Time in the market

Risk is often linked to the length of time you intend to hold your investments. It's 'time in the market not timing the market' that's important. For example, if you only want to invest for a short period of time (for instance, six months), a term deposit may be the way to go, especially if you're keen to get back your initial capital. With respect to investments like shares, real estate and managed funds, there's a risk you could lose money in the short term due to market volatility—they can go up and down like a yoyo. That's why these investments are generally considered to be medium- to long-term holdings (for instance, three to five years). So you may need to keep them for some considerable time before you're likely to see any noticeable return on your investment. This is especially the case with real estate, where you'll also have to take into account the high entry and exit costs that you'll need to recoup before you're likely to make a profit.

Handy tip

If you want to know more about managing investment risk the following websites may be worth examining:

⇒ National Australia Bank ‹www.nab.com.au› — go to 'Managing general investment risks'

⇒ Commonwealth Bank ‹www.commbank.com.au› — go to 'Managing investment risk'

⇒ Australian Super ‹www.australiansuper.com› — go to 'Investment basics — Managing risk'

⇒ Australian Securities and Investment Commission ‹www.asic.gov.au› — go to 'How do you manage your investment risks?'

Step 4: examine the tax issues

When you come to think about it every investment decision you make has a potential tax issue that you'll need to mull over (which is great news for tax consultants). This is because under Australian tax law you're liable to pay income tax on investment income you derive (such as interest, dividends and rent) and CGT if you make a capital gain on sale of your investment assets. To add salt to the wound there's also a 10 per cent goods and services tax (GST) slug on your purchases and sales. For example, this will occur if you buy a new property from a property developer. The impact of tax could also play a role as to when you should sell an investment asset and take some profit off the table. Under the CGT provisions if you buy and sell CGT assets such as shares, real estate and collectables within 12 months and you make a capital gain, the entire gain is liable to tax. (So you bear all the risks and the Tax Office shares the spoils—yuck!) But there is some relief. If you keep your CGT assets for more than 12 months and make a capital gain on sale, only half the gain is taxed. The other half is tax-free. In the meantime, if you incur expenses such as interest, rates, insurance and repairs in respect to income-producing assets you own, the outgoings are tax deductible (see chapters 9 and 13). Incidentally, you could gain some significant tax advantages such as franking credits if you own shares that pay franked dividends and a capital works deduction if you own an investment property. To add icing to the cake you could even receive a tax-free superannuation pension if you're over 60 years of age (see chapter 17).

There are also different ways you can structure your financial affairs to reduce the impact of taxation. For example, your capacity to split income (losses) and capital gains (losses) among family members; and paying no tax if you set up a superannuation retirement fund. A qualified accountant, tax consultant, solicitor or financial planner can help you select a suitable investment structure that's right for you. I discuss these issues in more detail in chapter 3.

Getting a tax benefit

Under Australian tax law there are anti–tax avoidance provisions to stop you from entering into certain contrived arrangements or schemes: that is, if the sole or dominant purpose is to obtain a tax benefit. There are also heavy fines if you're prosecuted and you may even be invited to spend some time in the slammer. There's an old saying that investment decisions should not be done solely to gain a tax benefit. Any tax savings flowing from an investment should be looked upon as a bonus rather than the primary reason for wanting to invest. You'll often find investment promoters pushing the tax angle to entice you to invest. For example, you can claim up-front tax deductions if you invest in forestry managed investment schemes; and you can get tax savings from negative-gearing a new property. Sounds great! But let's check whether the investment arrangement is likely to make you money first. It's no use getting a tax benefit if the arrangement turns out to be a dog. Further, the Tax Office isn't impressed with investors entering into 'wash sales'. These are arrangements where you sell shares predominantly to claim a capital loss (that can be deducted from a capital gain), and buy them back immediately. There're anti–tax avoidance provisions to stop you from doing this (see the Tax Office's *Taxpayer Alert TA 2008/7*).

Step 5: make sense of economic data

There's an old maxim that goes along the lines of 'a rising tide lifts all boats,' meaning when the general economy is booming most companies stand to benefit. The performance of many investments can often hinge on how domestic and overseas economies (especially the US) are faring. This is because the current state of the economy will tell you if company profits are likely to rise or fall; whether there is full employment; and whether people are spending all their hard-earned income (such as buying new cars and doing a lot of shopping). It'll also be a key indicator as to whether your investments are likely to grow and pay regular income.

Handy tip

During the earnings reporting season, which occurs around February and August, all the major Australian companies listed on the ASX will advise shareholders whether their profits (or losses) are rising or falling. This is also a key indicator of how the Australian economy is currently performing.

The major economic indicators that are often discussed in the media are:

$ the rate of inflation

$ interest rates

$ the value of the Australian dollar.

A key monetary policy of the Reserve Bank of Australia is to keep inflation below 3 per cent. This is done to help maintain steady economic growth and employment. Inflation moves up or down when the prices of a predetermined basket of goods and services go up or down. The consumer price index measures Australia's rate of inflation. For example, an upward movement will have an adverse impact on the purchasing power of the Australian dollar. And if it keeps going up, fixed-interest investors will soon find they can't buy the same things they could have purchased in the good old days. On the other hand, if interest rates increase, company profits and property valuations will tend to fall, as it will reduce consumer demand and make it more difficult for people to borrow money and repay debt.

With respect to movements in the Australia dollar, a rise or fall will affect Australian exports and imports. For example, a rising dollar will make exports more expensive, and the share prices of Australian exporting companies (for example, mining companies) will tend to fall. This is because sales will most likely fall as their products become more expensive to buy overseas. On the other hand, a decrease will make exports cheaper and imports more expensive. If you want to know more about the Australian economy the following websites may be worth examining:

$ Reserve Bank of Australia <www.rba.gov.au> — go to 'Latest News' and 'Rates & Statistics'

$ National Australia Bank <www.nabgroup.com> — go to 'Economic Commentary'

$ ANZ Bank <www.anz.com.au> — go to 'ANZ Economic Outlook'

$ Commonwealth Bank <www.commbank.com.au> — go to 'Economic Update'

$ Westpac Bank <www.westpac.com.au> — go to 'Economic Reports'.

The global financial crisis

When the US merchant bank Lehmann Brothers collapsed in September 2008 due to its heavy exposure to the subprime mortgage market, it was the spark that lit the global financial crisis. Within the blink of an eye, the US Dow Jones index plunged more than 40 per cent, millions of people were put out of work and the banking system stopped lending money. In Australia the S&P 200 index also fell sharply. Personal share portfolios plunged and superannuation fund balances fell significantly.

To restore confidence federal governments were forced to introduce stimulus packages to kick-start economic activity. They also had to guarantee bank accounts to stabilise the banking sector and to encourage banks to start lending again. By September 2009 there was light at the end of the tunnel. Economic confidence was stabilised and sharemarket valuations rose more than 40 per cent from their all-time lows. Those investors who were brave enough to have invested in the major blue-chip companies during this crisis period would have made a small fortune within a short period of time.

Shares versus real estate

Investing in the sharemarket and real estate are the two dominant ways of building wealth. At the end of the day your personal circumstances, preferences and risk profile could play a role as to which one you'll choose (or perhaps a bit of both might be the way to go). The following checklist provides a snapshot of how these investments compare with one another (I chat about these issues in more detail in later chapters):

$ *Income.* Both investment options can generate a reliable source of income for you—namely, dividends and rent. This is important to know if you're a retiree or an investor in need of additional income. When you take into account the dividend franking credits and the fact there are no ongoing costs, the yield your share portfolio can generate is generally higher than what you can get on a property investment.

$ *Capital growth.* Both investment options have the capacity to deliver capital growth, and will be the main sources you will be relying on to grow your wealth. Historically the sharemarket has generally outperformed the property market. But like a sudden tsunami, just when you think your share portfolio is making you heaps, it can virtually plunge in value overnight. For example, during the 2008–09 global financial meltdown the sharemarket fell more than 40 per cent in value within a short period of time, while property valuations remained relatively stable. So in the short term investing in shares can give you much heartache.

$ *Entry price.* With shares you can start off on a small scale using borrowings and savings and you can gradually build up as you become more affluent. With real estate you're virtually pushed into the deep end from the outset. Depending on which state or territory you reside the median price of property is now around $500 000. This means you may need to borrow a substantial sum and you could find yourself heavily in debt for a number of years.

$ *Entry costs.* The costs associated with buying shares are minimal and insignificant. Depending on how many shares you buy, the brokerage fees (and GST) would generally be no more than a few hundred dollars. With real estate, depending on which state or territory you reside in and how much you pay, the stamp duty, GST and legal costs you're likely to incur could be substantial (for example, $15 000 and $30 000). Unfortunately, this mind-boggling amount can be a major barrier to entry. So as soon as you buy a property you're already losing a truckload of money. And when you take into account selling costs, your property may need to increase more than $40 000 in value before you're likely to break even. To help ease the pain first home owners could qualify for a first home buyer's grant—subject to satisfying certain conditions.

$ *Ongoing costs.* When you own a share portfolio there are no ongoing costs. You can't say this about real estate. When you buy a property you're continually up for ongoing costs like land tax, rates, insurance and repairs, which could amount to thousands of dollars each year. Fortunately, these expenses are tax deductible if the property generates income.

$ *Liquidity.* The great thing about shares is they can be sold in a matter of seconds, and you'll get your money back within a few days. It's also possible for you to make a quick profit if share prices rise. Property, on the other hand, could take months to sell, and you can only sell a property if you can find a buyer who's willing to pay the price you're asking. This could become a major concern if you've got a property worth $500 000 that no-one wants, and you need the funds urgently.

$ *Flexibility.* You can sell small parcels of shares at the drop of a hat. Unfortunately, you can't do it with real estate (you can't ring up your real estate agent and try to sell off one of your rooms!). However, it's possible for you to subdivide and sell off part of the land you own.

$ *Portability.* You can put your entire share portfolio in your briefcase and take it with you if you move interstate or overseas (and any dividends you receive can be credited directly into your bank account). Unfortunately, you can't take your properties with you if you decide to go elsewhere. You may need to find someone and pay them for the privilege of collecting the rent and paying all the bills while you're away. If any major issues were to arise it could cost a packet trying to solve the problem from afar.

$ *Tax benefits.* There are significant tax benefits if you buy shares that pay dividends that are franked. A franked dividend means the company has paid tax on its profits and when this happens you get a franking credit. Franking credits are tax offsets that you can apply against the net tax payable on dividends (and other income) you derive. If you're a low income earner any excess franking credits will be refunded back to you, and the return on your investment will increase. With respect to real estate there are significant tax benefits from owning an income-producing property, such as depreciation deductions and a capital works deduction. The federal government has also introduced the first home saving accounts where it will contribute money to help you save for a deposit. Any interest derived will be taxed at the rate of 15 per cent! To add icing to the cake any capital gains you make on sale of your main residence is totally exempt from tax (see chapter 14). The downside is if you make a capital loss you will not be able to make use of it as the property is exempt.

$ *Exit charges.* As is the case when you buy shares, the costs associated with selling them are minimal and insignificant. At worst your brokerage fees (and GST) would generally be no more than a few hundred dollars. When you sell a property you will normally consult a real estate agent. Their fees are normally 2.5 per cent of the sale price. So if the sale price is $500 000 it will cost you around $12 500 to sell it, plus other costs such as advertising expenses (normally around $1000) and any repairs to make your property appealing to a potential buyer.

Attending get-rich-quick seminars

I love going to free investment seminars (with my bag of pop-corn!) that show you how to 'get rich quick' for very little effort (and — wait for it — 'no prior experience is necessary'). With the aid of a slick PowerPoint presentation, trained financial gurus wearing their latest Versace outfits explain how the scheme works and how they became instant millionaires from participating. But wait, there's more. At the conclusion of the seminar if you stay around, you can sip some free champagne and speak to them on a one-to-one basis. Alternatively, if you have to leave early they're even willing to come to your home if you need additional information (now that's what I call dedication!). I often wonder why these humanitarians are willing to go out of their way to help me become a wealthy person!

Examining the facts

Get-rich-quick investment seminars are normally associated with:

$ *flogging complex investment schemes in complex investment structures that offer an attractive rate of return — 'earn up to 20 per cent per annum'.* Although the 'earn up to' rate of return may sound attractive, keep in mind the old investment adage discussed previously, 'the higher the rate the higher the risk'. The sceptic in me would say, if this is such a great investment, why are they willing to share it with me. If you find the arrangement is complex or difficult to understand, the answer is quite simple: don't invest!

$ *buying a negatively geared property from a property developer.* Although the tax benefits from negative gearing a property may look attractive, it pays to check whether the purchase price is a true reflection of its market value. You should always consult an independent professional to ensure you're not paying more than what the property is actually worth (which is often the case), especially if it's located in another state or country. I cover how negative gearing works in chapter 4.

$ *claiming upfront tax deductions.* As a matter of course, you should check whether the Australian Taxation Office has issued any 'product ruling' to confirm these assertions and all the conditions you may need to satisfy. You should also check whether the ATO has issued any 'taxpayer alerts'. According to the ATO website: 'Taxpayer alerts are intended to be an early warning of our concerns about significant and emerging potential aggressive tax planning issues or arrangements that the ATO has under risk assessment'.

$ *investing in a new managed investment scheme.* By law all licensed investment scheme promoters must prepare a product disclosure statement or prospectus setting out the relevant information you'll need to know. So it's important that you read these legal documents carefully and understand what you're doing. If in doubt you should immediately contact the Australian Securities &

Investments Commission and seek its advice or contact a qualified financial planner.

$ *flogging expensive share courses and software packages that can plot share price movements and (wait for it) miraculously predict the future* (enough said!).

Handy tip

The Tax Office has issued two handy fact sheets, *Investment Checklist* and *Investment Warnings*, that explain what you should do before you commit yourself in any managed investment schemes. If you want these fact sheets you can contact your local ATO or you can download them from the Tax Office website ‹www.ato.gov.au›.

When promoters market these types of schemes, they're always eager to emphasise the positives, and will produce persuasive data to support their assertions (which sounds great if everything goes according to plan). Unfortunately, the sceptic in me would rather hear the negatives and what happens if the opposite were to occur. To win you over they're even prepared to offer you immediate finance ('just sign here!').

If you come across these get-rich-quick schemes, don't make any spur of the moment decisions that you may live to regret, and don't sign any documents. It's amazing how many people are instantly won over at the conclusion of each 'live show' (especially the negative-gearing seminars). If you're keen to participate it's prudent that you consult an independent professional first and carefully examine the facts and possible risks you're taking.

Handy tip

ASIC has on its website ‹www.fido.gov.au› a section called 'Scams & warnings' that may be worth a look. It's no use doing this exercise once you've parted with your money.

Making a decision

Before you sign on the dotted line it pays to check the following key points:

$ *Does it pay a regular income flow?* Keep in mind if the investment doesn't generate regular income, there's a risk you may be denied a tax deduction. This could become a major concern if you're paying a substantial amount of interest and ongoing commissions and fees. As a general rule, you can only claim a tax deduction if there's a reasonable expectation that you'll derive income. If in doubt you should immediately consult a tax professional or seek a private ruling from the ATO. It's no use doing this after the horse has bolted.

$ *Will the investment generate capital growth?* If you have to wait many years to find out, there's a risk it may not eventuate. Further, you should check out the tax consequences if the investment fails to live up to expectations (for example, is any potential loss a loss of income that can be claimed as a tax deduction, or a capital loss that can only be deducted from a capital gain?). Again, if in doubt you should consult a tax professional or seek a private ruling from the ATO.

$ *Is there an established market?* You should check whether you can get your initial capital back if you want to get out early; who the likely buyers are; and who sets the market price at the time of sale. If there's no secondary market (as is often the case with managed investment schemes), you could find yourself stuck with an investment that no-one wants. (I love hearing the feeble explanations you're given when there's no ready market to offload these investments!).

$ *What are the ongoing fees?* If upfront costs, commissions and ongoing fees are payable, you need to know how they're calculated and why you have to pay them. This could become a major concern if you're not receiving income or the investment turns out to be a dud. Again, check out the possible tax consequences of incurring these outlays before you commit yourself.

So if you plan to go to one of these seminars, you may see me in the front row eating my popcorn and enjoying the 'live show'. It's better than watching television!

Chapter 3

Who is in command? Ownership structures

Finding the right investment that's going to make you a truckload of money is only half the battle. You also have to weigh up the commercial and taxation issues that go with owning an investment. Before you sign on the dotted line make sure you understand what you're doing. If you change your mind or make a mistake after you commit yourself it could cost you dearly—plus cause a lot of pain and heartache—trying to fix up the mess.

So if you're not sure what to do you should get professional help. Remember it pays to be safe rather than sorry. In this chapter I chat about the different ways you can own investments and the tax issues that could affect your decision.

Five ways to own an investment

Before you buy an investment you should give serious consideration to the different legal ways you can structure your financial affairs. This is because there are many commercial and taxation benefits you can tap into (see following). There are also disadvantages that may not appeal to you. So before you sign any legal documents it may be a prudent move to get professional advice from a financial planner, solicitor and/or tax consultant.

The various legal ways you can structure your financial affairs will affect:

$ the commercial and tax constraints you'll need to follow in respect to owning investment assets in different ownership structures

$ the ongoing costs you're likely to incur each year (for instance, accounting fees)

$ your capacity to access capital gains tax concessions (companies miss out on the CGT 50 per cent discount)

$ the amount of tax deductions you can claim each year

$ your legal capacity to split income and losses (individuals can't split with family members)

$ your capacity to access tax losses you may incur each year (companies and trusts can't distribute losses)

$ the likely division of wealth from a marriage breakup; pre-nuptial agreements

$ your capacity to protect your assets from potential creditors: a major concern if you're running a business

$ your capacity to quickly terminate the legal structure you have set up: it can be complex and costly.

Generally, there are five main ways you can own an investment. The structure you select will depend on your personal circumstances and what you wish to achieve. They are:

1 outright ownership

2 joint ownership

3 company

4 trust

5 complying superannuation fund.

> **Handy tip**
>
> It's possible for you to have a combination of investment structures (for instance, a trust and company) tailored to suit your particular circumstances. As these types of structures can be complex and costly to administer you should seek professional advice from a solicitor or accountant.

Outright ownership

The great bit about owning an investment asset outright is you can do whatever you want with it. The good news gets even better as you get to keep all the income your investments derive and any capital gains you make on sale. With respect to capital gains, only 50 per cent is liable to be taxed if you own an investment asset for more than 12 months! This is not the case if the investment is held in a company structure. But wait, there's more. You can claim all the expenses you incur in deriving investment income such as interest to buy investment assets that pay income. And if you incur a capital loss you can deduct it from any capital gains you make.

Before you start celebrating, the trade-off is you'll have to declare all the income in your individual tax return and pay tax plus a Medicare levy. What's annoying here is you can't split any investment income or capital gains you make with family members. And to add insult to injury if you transfer ownership to someone else (for example, to a family member or to your self managed super fund), you could be liable to pay capital gains tax. This is because there will be a change in ownership.

Handy tip

If you own a property (outright or jointly) that's your main residence, any capital gain you make on sale is exempt from tax. This is not the case if your main residence is owned by a company or trust.

Taking advantage of the poor

During one of my training courses a disheartened participant informed me that as she didn't work and had no money, she was wasting her time learning about wealth creation. In order not to lose her confidence I had to quickly find her a reason for being there. When she told me she was married I advised her that her husband was in an excellent position to exploit her situation. This is because if he buys investments — such as shares — in her name, he'll be able to take advantage of her low-income threshold. Under Australian tax law an individual can earn up to $16 000 before they're liable to pay tax (per 2010–11 tax rates). And if he contributes $3000 to a complying superannuation fund on her behalf, he will qualify for a $540 tax offset. When she heard this she was eager to learn as she had found her motivation to invest.

Joint ownership

Owning investments jointly (for example, husband and wife) is similar to owning them outright with each joint owner having an equal say. Under Australian tax law if you are in receipt of income jointly you will be considered to be in partnership. Incidentally, a partnership does not pay tax on the income it derives as all income (and losses) must be distributed to the individual partners. The great bit about this is your ability to split the income and any capital gain you make among the joint owners in accordance to their legal entitlement. This means you're only liable to pay tax on the share you receive. If you get joint investment income such as interest, dividends and rent, you don't have to lodge a partnership tax return. But you will have to declare your share in your individual tax return. By the way, if your taxable income is less than $16 000 no tax is payable on this amount. Joint owners are also eligible for the 50 per cent CGT discount if you make a capital gain on sale of investments owned for more than 12 months. Another plus is any losses you incur (for instance, from negative gearing a rental property) can be deducted from other assessable income you derive. This isn't the case if the investment is owned in a company or trust structure, as these losses cannot be distributed. A major setback is your inability to distribute all the income and capital gains to one joint owner (for example, to the person who pays the least amount of tax). And you can't distribute all the losses to the joint owner who is likely to benefit the most from such a distribution. All distributions must be in accordance with your legal entitlement, which is normally done on a 50–50 basis.

Handy tip

If you own a property as 'joint tenants' (for example, husband and wife), and a joint tenant dies, the deceased's interest in the property automatically passes to the surviving joint tenant. This is not the case if the property is owned as 'tenants in common', which normally arises where both parties are not related (for instance, business partners). Under these circumstances you can nominate who should receive your legal entitlement to the property in your will.

Company

Under commercial law a company is a separate legal entity. This means it can own investments like shares and real estate in its own right. It also has limited liability so if a company gets into financial difficulty any potential shareholders' losses are limited to the value of their shares in the company. Under Australian tax law a company pays a 30 per cent rate of tax on the net profit it derives. A major benefit of having a company structure is it doesn't have to distribute dividends to its shareholders; and if it does distribute dividends it can choose the right time to do so. Unfortunately, there are a number of disadvantages of owning investment assets in a company structure that may not appeal to you (especially when you examine the capital gains tax limitations). This is because:

$ company profits derived from all sources (for instance, investment income, exempt profits and capital gains) are taxed as dividends when they're distributed to shareholders. This is because a company can only distribute dividends to shareholders. However, shareholders will receive franking credits if the dividends are franked.

$ companies can't pick and choose which shareholders should receive company profits as is the case with a family trust structure. Dividend distributions are normally made in proportion to the number of shares you own. For example, if you own 40 per cent of the company you will get 40 per cent of any distribution the company makes.

$ shareholders are unable to access company losses. Losses must remain within the company structure and can only be deducted from future company profits. This could become a major heartburn if a company is negative gearing an investment property or share portfolio, and incurring substantial losses that shareholders can't access. If you think this could be the case it may be more beneficial to own those investment assets in joint names, as you will be able to access those losses each year.

$ a major drawback of a company structure is a company is ineligible to claim a 50 per cent CGT discount benefit on disposal of investment assets owned for more than 12 months. This is not the case if the investment is held by an individual, in joint names or in a trust structure. So if you're planning on holding a property or shares for a number of years, a company structure may not be the way to go. This is because you will miss out on the 50 per cent discount if you make a capital gain on sale.

$ a company is ineligible for a main residence exemption (even if the shareholders were to reside in the property). This is because only individuals can own a main residence. This means the property is liable to CGT when it's subsequently sold. To add insult to injury you'll also miss out on the 50 per cent CGT discount if the property is held for more than 12 months (double ouch!).

$ as companies pay a 30 per cent flat rate of tax it could be bad news if the marginal tax rate of all the shareholders is 15 per cent or less. This could arise if your taxable is less than $37 000 (per 2010–11 tax rates).

$ companies miss out on the $6000 tax-free threshold that is available to individual investors. Companies effectively pay 30 per cent tax on the entire net profit they derive.

$ your annual accounting and administration costs could be substantial and there are complex rules you'll need to comply with if you want to terminate the company.

Trust

One popular way of owning investments is to set up a trust, particularly a family discretionary trust. A trust is a legal obligation binding a person (the trustee) who has control over investment assets (for instance, shares and property) for the benefit of beneficiaries. The great bit about having a family discretionary trust is the trustee has discretion as to how the trust net income should be distributed to the beneficiaries (normally family members). A trustee can distribute trust net income to specific beneficiaries to meet their individual needs, which can change from year to year. Unfortunately, you can't do this if the investments are held in joint names or in a company structure. For example, if the beneficiaries were a spouse who doesn't work and a child who attends full-time university, it's possible to distribute $16 000 to each person and not pay any tax (per 2010–11 tax rates). This is because no tax is payable if your taxable income is below $16 000. The trade-off here is a trust cannot distribute losses to beneficiaries. As is the case with companies, a trust is ineligible for a main residence exemption (even if the beneficiaries were to reside in the property). This means the property is not exempt from capital gains tax if it is subsequently sold.

Handy tip

Income flowing through a trust will retain its character or identity when the trustee makes a distribution to the beneficiaries. So if the trustee distributes rent or an exempt capital gain it will be rent or an exempt capital gain in the hands of the beneficiary. This is not the case if a distribution is made by a company. As mentioned previously, this is because companies can only pay dividends to its shareholders.

As is the case with a partnership structure, the trust is not liable to pay tax on the trust net income it derives. Instead, the income is assessed to either the trustee or beneficiaries. By law once the trustee has calculated the trust net income, the trustee must find out:

$ who are the beneficiaries

$ whether any beneficiary is 'presently entitled' to receive a trust distribution

$ whether any beneficiary is 'under a legal disability' (for instance, because the person is under the age of 18).

If a beneficiary is presently entitled to receive a trust distribution (meaning they have a legal right to demand the payment) the income is assessed to them. This means the beneficiary is personally liable to pay tax on the amount they receive. However, if a beneficiary is presently entitled but is under a legal disability, the trustee is liable to pay the tax. The trustee is also liable to pay tax if no beneficiaries are presently entitled or the trustee decides not to make a distribution.

Setting up a trust is great if all the beneficiaries are adults (in Australia you're considered to be an adult once you turn 18 years of age). Problems can arise if the trustee were to make a distribution to a minor beneficiary who is under a legal disability. When this happens the trustee is liable to pay a special rate of tax commonly known as Division 6AA (see table 3.1). This is an anti-avoidance provision to discourage trustees from distributing unearned income such as interest dividends and rent to children under the age of 18. But there is some relief. Minor beneficiaries can claim a low income tax offset. When this is applied they can receive up to $3333 (in 2010–11) before the special rate of tax kicks in. It may not sound much but I suppose it's better than nothing.

Table 3.1: Division 6AA — special rate of tax

Taxable income	Rate of tax
$0–$416	Nil tax payable
$417–$1307	66% of excess over $416
Above $1307	45% on entire amount of taxable income

Case study: receiving a trust distribution

The trustee of the Crabtree family discretionary trust calculated the trust net income to be $60 000. The trust has two beneficiaries named Jack and Jill.

At the end of the financial year the trustee distributed $16 000 to Jill (who is over 18 years of age), $10 000 to Jack (who is five years of age) and decided to retain and reinvest the balance ($34 000) to buy more shares. This is how the $60 000 trust net income is taxed:

⇒ *Distribution to Jill ($16 000)*. Because Jill is over 18 years of age she is presently entitled to the trust distribution and is under no legal disability. This means she is personally liable to pay tax on the $16 000 she received. If this is her sole source of income no tax is payable.

⇒ *Distribution to Jack ($10 000)*. As Jack is presently entitled to the trust distribution but is under a legal disability (because he is five years of age), the trustee is liable to pay tax on the $10 000 distribution. Under these circumstances the trustee is personally liable to pay a special rate of tax (see table 3.1).

⇒ *Amount retained and reinvested ($34 000)*. The $34 000 that had not been distributed is 'income to which no beneficiary is presently entitled'. In this case the trustee is personally liable to pay tax on this amount at the top marginal rate of tax plus a Medicare levy (currently 46.5 per cent).

Investments held by a child

A child under 18 years of age can own an investment (for instance, shares or a bank account) in their own name, or, as is usually the case, in trust, with the trustee normally being the child's parent. The Australian Tax Office has issued two fact sheets titled *Children's savings accounts* and *Children's share investment* to explain the tax issues associated with children deriving investment income. You can download a copy from the Tax Office website ‹www.ato.gov.au›.

Complying superannuation fund

A complying superannuation fund is an investment structure that allows you to accumulate wealth creation investment assets, such as shares and real estate, to help fund your retirement. The great news here is there are many benefits from putting money into a super fund (see chapter 15). Incidentally, the reason why it's called a 'complying' superannuation fund is because you have to follow strict rules if you want to tap into these benefits. One nasty rule is you can't withdraw any money until you reach your preservation age and retire. This will normally occur when you reach 60 years of age. So you may have to wait many years before you can access your money. But the wait could prove worthwhile. This is because once you turn 60 years of age and retire all withdrawals—whether you take it as a pension or cash—are entirely exempt from tax! I chat about this in more detail in chapter 17. In the meantime, while you're in the accumulation phase you will find:

$ complying superannuation funds pay tax at the rate of 15 per cent. The tax bill can be effectively reduced to nil if you invest in shares that pay fully franked dividends (see chapter 9).

$ there are attractive tax incentives to encourage you to make a contribution. For example, if you're self-employed you can claim a tax deduction if you make a concessional contribution. There are also tax incentives to encourage low income earners to put money into a superannuation fund such as the federal government co-contribution scheme (see chapter 15).

$ pensions payable to individuals aged 55 to 59 qualify for a 15 per cent tax offset, and of course once you turn 60 all payments are exempt from tax.

Running a small business

Under the CGT concessions for small business, if you operate a small business and you make a capital gain on sale of 'active business assets', the gain can be reduced to nil. This means you won't have to pay any tax! These concessions are available to sole traders, a partner in a partnership, a company and trust. So everyone who runs a small business can potentially benefit provided you satisfy certain conditions. Active business assets are assets you own and use in running your business, for example, your business premises. (By the way, these concessions are not available if your business structure owns an investment property that derives passive income such as rent).

If your business is operated through a company or trust and the business asset is a share or interest in a trust, you'll need to pass the '20 per cent significant individual test', to qualify for these concessions. This test checks whether an individual has at least a 20 per cent 'small business participation percentage' in respect to voting rights and profit and capital distributions. This could become an important issue to consider if you're planning to set up a company or trust, as a maximum of five 'significant individuals' can gain this benefit.

One small business concession is the 'CGT 15-year exemption concession'. This applies to individuals who have been in business for at least 15 years. Under this concession any capital gain you make on sale of active business assets is exempt from tax. To qualify you'll need to have owned the asset for at least 15 years and you must be over 55 years of age and retired. This could prove a good way of building up wealth, because once you turn 55 years of age the tax-free proceeds can be used to help fund your retirement.

For a comprehensive discussion on all the conditions you'll need to satisfy, the Tax Office has issued a publication titled *Am I eligible for the small business entity concessions?* You can download a copy from its website ‹www.ato.gov.au›.

Chapter 4

Borrowing to build wealth

We've all heard the saying 'opportunity only knocks once'. Well, no truer words have been spoken when it comes to wealth creation. As they say in the classics, you've got to be in it to win it. Generally, there are two ways to buy wealth creation assets like shares and real estate. You can either save until you've got the money or you can borrow. If you save it could take many years to get the ball rolling. And you may find yourself in the classic dog-chasing-its-tail scenario if the investments you're keen to buy are continually rising. Borrowing, on the other hand, gives you the opportunity to invest now; especially if you can get in at bargain-basement prices. In this chapter I chat about the nuts and bolts of borrowing money to build wealth.

Getting a loan

It goes without saying you need money to make money. To kick-start the process you'll have to convince your bank manager—financial institution—why you need a loan and what you plan to do with it. So when you pay them a visit you'll need to provide a statement of all your personal assets and liabilities, details of your income and expenses, your employment history, and what security (guarantees) you can offer them (see chapter 1). This is to check whether you have the capacity to repay the loan. Keep in mind penalties will apply if you're unable to meet your financial commitments by the due date. When you take out a loan you will most likely incur the following fees and charges:

$ loan establishment fees to set up the loan

$ ongoing service fees and transaction fees

$ early repayment fees if you pay back the loan too early

$ default fees if you're unable to meet your loan commitments.

> **Handy tip**
>
> If you want to know more about getting finance visit the Australian Securities and Investments Commission website ‹www.fido.gov.au› and go to 'About financial products' and click on 'Loans & credit'.

Choosing a loan: the more the merrier

There are many types of loans you can take out to suit your particular needs and circumstances. The common ones you can consider are listed here:

$ *Interest-only loans.* Where you're only required to repay the interest over a certain period of time. The principal is repaid at a later date or when the loan matures. The rate of interest can be fixed, variable or a combination of both. The great bit here is the interest payments on investment loans are tax deductible!

$ *Principal and interest loans.* Where you'll pay back both interest and principal at regular intervals (for example, fortnightly or monthly). The rate of interest charged can be fixed, variable or a combination of both.

$ *Fixed-rate loans.* Where the rate of interest is fixed for a certain period of time (for example, 7 per cent). In the meantime, if interest rates start to rocket upwards (for example, up to 10 per cent), you won't be up for any additional interest repayments. The benefit here is you'll know exactly how much interest you have to pay each week, fortnight or month, and you can budget and plan ahead with certainty. The bad news is if interest rates fall (for example, down to 4 per cent), you're stuck with the higher rate, and you can't increase or decrease your repayments. There are stiff penalties (for example, 'break costs') if you try to switch from a fixed-rate loan to a variable-rate loan.

$ *Variable-rate loans.* Where the rate of interest will vary in line with the prevailing market. This is great news if interest rates fall as you'll pay less interest. But if interest rates were go through the roof, your interest repayments will rise accordingly. An added bonus here is you can pay back more than the required minimum, and you can pay off the loan at a faster rate. It goes without saying the quicker you can repay your loan the less interest you'll incur.

$ *Home loans.* Where you can access funds to buy your main residence. The loan will have specific features tailored to suit your personal needs. The rate of interest charged can be fixed, variable or a combination of both. Home loan mortgage rates fluctuate in line with the Reserve Bank of Australia's cash rate (which affects market interest rates). Some of the features you can get are:

- redraw facility or line of credit—where you can access funds to buy investments

- interest offset facility—where your savings account is linked to your home loan

- portability—where you can transfer your loan between properties

- split loans—part home loan, part investment loan.

$ *Split loans.* Where interest charges are partly fixed and partly variable to suit your particular circumstances. It can also be a loan that is partly a home loan and partly an investment loan. When taking out a part home loan, part investment loan there are special rules you'll need to follow in respect to claiming an interest deduction. (For more details read the Australian Taxation Office fact sheet *Split loan interest deductions*).

$ *Line of credit loans.* Where you can access finance up to an approved, predetermined limit (for example, up to $60 000). You will normally offer property as security and it's possible for you to borrow as much as 85 per cent of the value of your property. These loans give you the capacity to access cash at short notice (see case study: positive gearing a share portfolio, page 66).

$ *Bridging loans.* These are normally short-term loans to cover your financial position while another financial transaction is in the course of being completed. For instance, you need funds to buy a property now while waiting to receive the net proceeds from a property you've just sold.

$ *Reverse mortgage loans.* These loans allow borrowers over a certain age (for instance, 60) who own property to draw down cash. No repayments are necessary until the property is sold. If the borrower were to die any outstanding amount is recouped from the estate.

$ *Low doc loans.* Where no documentary evidence is required to verify your capacity to repay the loan. They're normally offered to high-risk investors at a high rate of interest. The downside here is the rate of interest is usually significantly higher than other loans, and you risk forfeiting your security (for instance, property) if you're unable to meet your loan repayments.

$ *Vendor finance loans.* Where the vendor provides the necessary finance to the purchaser to buy a property (for instance, from a property developer).

$ *Margin loans.* Used to fund a share portfolio where you'll use a combination of your own capital and borrowings from a financial institution (see margin lending later in this chapter for more details).

$ *Capital protection loans.* Used to buy shares where you can protect yourself from incurring a loss if your shares fall in value. These are normally non-recourse loans where the lender rather than the investor suffers any potential loss. Under Australian tax law there is a limit on the amount of interest you can claim as a tax deduction. If you want to know more about these loans see the Taxation Office fact sheet *How are capital protected products and borrowings treated?*

$ *Personal loans.* These are normally unsecured loans that you can take out for a specific purpose (for instance, to buy a car or shares). These loans can be structured as fixed- or variable-rate loans and your repayments can be weekly, fortnightly or monthly.

$ *Credit cards.* These are unsecured loans that allow you to access cash up to a predetermined limit (for instance, you need instant cash or to pay for items you purchased). You will incur a high rate of interest.

Looking at five key issues

So you've got your loan approved and you're itching to grow your wealth. Before you commit yourself and sign on the dotted line, there are five key issues associated with investment loans that you'll to need to consider first. This is because if you get any of these wrong you could find yourself going backwards.

$ *Investment growth.* When you borrow money to buy wealth creation assets like shares and real estate, there's an implied assumption that they'll increase in value (which is great if it happens!) But first a word of caution: although they can deliver capital growth, the tricky bit here is there is a risk that they can also fall in value. Unfortunately, there are no cast-iron guarantees that you'll always come out in front. So it's crucial that you invest your money wisely. Remember, if valuations fall you'll be paying off a loan that's not increasing your wealth (which defeats the purpose of investing). This was a major concern in the United States when property prices fell sharply in 2007. Property owners found the value of their property used to secure a loan had fallen below the amount they initially borrowed (commonly known as 'negative equity').

$ *Income.* It's important that you check whether the investment you plan to buy will generate an income stream (for instance, interest, dividends and rent). This is because under Australian tax law you can only claim a tax deduction if your investment assets (such as shares or a rental property) generate income (see 'negative gearing' later in this chapter). Also, the income you derive can help you service your loan repayments.

$ *Interest rates.* When you borrow money from a financial institution you're liable to pay interest and charges. Loans are normally structured as fixed- or variable-rate loans or a combination of both. It's also possible to get an interest-only loan where you only pay interest. The difficult bit about all these types of loan arrangements is choosing the right balance and paying the least amount of interest. So it's important that you understand what you're doing.

$ *Cash flow.* When you borrow money you'll enter into a legal obligation to repay the loan plus interest within a given period (for example, 10 years). So make sure you have a sufficient cash flow (ready cash) to meet your loan commitments as they fall due. Otherwise, penalties will apply and there's a risk you could forfeit your investment assets.

$ *Taxation deductions.* Make sure you buy investment assets that generate income, otherwise your interest payments are not tax deductible. Also, you must be deriving assessable income (for instance, salary and wages, business profits and investment income) in order to claim a tax deduction. The tax you'll save depends on the amount of taxable income you derive and your marginal rate of tax (which can vary between 0 per cent and 45 per cent). For example, if your marginal rate of tax is 30 per cent, for every dollar you claim as a tax deduction you'll effectively save 30 cents in tax. Keep in mind once your taxable income is below $16 000 no tax is payable. Incidentally, taxable income is total assessable income less allowable deductions.

Subprime mortgage crisis

The subprime mortgage crisis happened in the United States as a result of indiscriminate lending to high-risk borrowers to buy property ('subprime market'). These subprime loans were dubbed NINJA loans because many of the borrowers had 'No Income No Job No Assets'. These high-risk mortgage-backed loans were bundled up and sold to US and overseas financial institutions. When US property prices began to decline in value in 2007 many borrowers who were unemployed and unable to meet their loan repayments were evicted from their properties. These mortgage-backed loans subsequently fell in value and virtually became worthless in the balance sheets of the financial institutions that held them. Financial institutions immediately stopped lending money and all the stock markets throughout the world fell sharply. The collapse of the subprime mortgage market was the primary cause of the global financial crisis in 2008–09.

Handy tip

Under the CGT provisions non-deductible interest can be added in the investment asset's cost base, and can be used to reduce any capital gain that's liable to tax (see chapter 13).

Negative gearing

A major selling point investment promoters love emphasising to potential investors is the tax benefits that flow from negative gearing (see chapter 2). If the purpose of the loan is to buy an investment asset that pays income (for instance, shares and real estate), the interest payments are tax deductible. So it's important that you check there's a reasonable expectation that you'll receive income such as interest dividends and rent. The bad news here is if you borrow to buy non–income producing assets (such as your home or shares in companies that don't declare dividends), your interest payments are not tax deductible.

This is how negative gearing works: if your total allowable expenses (which will be predominantly interest) exceed the investment income you derive (such as dividends and rent), you can deduct the net investment loss from other assessable income you derive (such as salary and wages). The great thing about doing this is you'll save paying tax on the other income you derive! So it's important that you have another source of income to claim the investment loss, otherwise the tax benefit is effectively lost. This will happen if your taxable income is below $16000, because no tax is payable once your taxable income falls below this amount.

If you're contemplating negative gearing keep in mind your investment asset must increase in value. Otherwise, you could quickly find yourself with the ugly prospect of paying off an investment asset that's decreasing in value, and generating a negative cash flow. This could easily happen if you intend to purchase a share portfolio where share prices fluctuate daily.

Case study: negative gearing a property

Seven years ago Deepa borrowed $300000 — interest rate 7.5 per cent variable — to finance the purchase of a new property that she intended to lease. The purchase price was $500000. She was told at the time she bought the property that the building's construction costs were $200000. As the building was constructed after September 1987 Deepa can claim a 2.5 per cent per annum capital works deduction (see chapter 13). The amount of salary and wages she derived was $60000 and her marginal rate of tax plus the Medicare levy is 31.5 per cent.

Case study *(cont'd)*: negative gearing a property

At the end of the financial year Deepa's accounting records provided the following information:

⇒ gross rent received $18750

⇒ interest payments on loan $22500

⇒ annual rental expenditure $3500

⇒ depreciation deduction $4300

⇒ capital works deduction $5000

Deepa's real estate agent has advised her that the property's market value is currently $900000.

Calculations:

Gross rent received	$18750

Less deductions:	
Interest payments on loan	$22500
Annual rental expenditure	$3500
Depreciation deduction	$4300
Capital works deduction	$5000
Total deductions	**$35300**
Net loss	**$16550**

As Deepa incurred a $16550 tax loss from negative gearing her property, the tax loss can be deducted from the $60000 salary and wages she derived as illustrated below:

Salary and wages	$60000
Less net loss from rent	$16550
Taxable income	**$43450**

As Deepa's marginal rate of tax (plus Medicare levy) is 31.5 per cent, she will gain a tax saving amounting to $5213 ($16550 × 31.5% = $5213). When she adds up all her total cash inflows (rent and tax saving) and deducts the amount from all her cash outflows (cash expenses), the shortfall Deepa will need to meet is $2037 (or $39 per week) as illustrated below:

Cash flow statement

Cash inflow	Gross rent	$18 750
	Tax saved	$5 213
		$23 963
Cash outflow	Interest payment	$22 500
	Rental expenditure	$3 500
		$26 000
Net cash outlay		**$2 037**

(As the depreciation deductions and capital works deductions are not cash outlays they are not included in the cash flow statement.)

So for a net cash outlay of $39 per week, Deepa is paying off a property that had effectively increased from $500 000 to $900 000 in value over a seven year period (Ah! Building wealth and loving it.)

Positive gearing: oh what fun!

During one of my wealth creation courses a participant was very eager to learn about negative gearing. When I told her it was possible to 'positive gear' she was totally unimpressed. According to her way of thinking the only way to go was to negative gear (the buzz word commonly associated with wealth creation). When you negative gear you're effectively losing money (as illustrated in the previous case study). So to restore the balance your investment must increase in value. This is to compensate you for the negative cash outflows you're incurring while paying off the loan.

Wherever possible you should endeavour to positive gear. When you positive gear the investment income you derive will cover all your borrowing costs. And—wait for it—you won't need to use any of your own funds to service the loan (as is the case when you're negative gearing). To add icing to the cake, if your investment increases in value you will be laughing all the way to the bank (see case study following). Positive gearing is worth considering if you can take out an interest-only loan, especially when interest rates are low. Provided your investment income covers all your outlays (your interest payments and other expenses you incur), and your investment increases in value, you will be virtually making money without raising a finger, so to speak. Positive gearing works great with shares as illustrated in the following case study.

Case study: positive gearing a share portfolio

Pauline has established a line of credit with her local bank. The account credit limit is $60 000 and the interest rate is 7 per cent per annum payable at the end of each month. She is keen to buy 2000 CBA shares which had plunged from around $61 per share to $26.50 because of the global financial crisis. On 2 February 2009 she purchased 2000 CBA shares @ $26.50 per share — total outlay $53 000. Shortly after she bought them, CBA declared a $1.13 interim dividend payable on 23 March 2009 — total payment $2260. Six months later CBA declared a $1.15 final dividend payable on 1 October 2009 — total payment $2300. On the debit side between 1 February 2009 and 1 October 2009 Pauline's interest payments amounted to $2800. When she deducted the total dividend payments ($4560) from her total interest payments ($2800) she was $1760 ahead! As Pauline's cash inflows (dividends) exceeded her cash outflows (interest) she was positive gearing. To add icing to the cake, when she found the market price of CBA on 1 October 2009 was $50.90 per share, she was $48 800 ahead! How easy is this, she thought! (Building wealth and loving it even more!).

Margin lending

One popular way to fund a share portfolio (or managed funds) is margin lending, where you'll use a combination of your own capital and borrowings. Under this arrangement a margin lender will lend money up to a certain amount (for instance $70 000) to buy approved Australian Securities Exchange–listed companies. The interest you'll incur is a tax deductible expense (provided the shares you buy pay dividends). In return you'll be required to pledge some of your own capital (for instance $30 000) in shares and/or cash. The maximum limit of the loan — referred to as a loan-to-valuation ratio (LVR) — is normally set at 70 per cent. This could prove a great way to create wealth if the shares you select increase in value. It's possible for you to make heaps if everything goes your way (plus receive dividends).

However, what happens if share valuations fall? The risk here is you could be up for a margin call, where you'll be required to inject additional securities (shares and/or cash) to cover the fall in value and to restore the LVR (see the case study following). To keep the margin lender happy you'll need to do this pronto, which normally means within 24 hours. Unfortunately, you're not permitted to ride out the storm until the market recovers. If you can't find the necessary amount, the securities you pledged will be sold and you could incur a substantial loss. This could become a major concern if share valuations are continually falling and you're liable for ongoing margin calls.

To avoid being constantly pestered with a margin call, the borrower will normally offer you a 'buffer' (for instance, 5 per cent). This is to allow for small daily fluctuations in the sharemarket. It's only when share valuations fall below the buffer that you'll be up for a margin call. There are certain strategies you can use to reduce your exposure to a margin call; for example, borrow less than the maximum permitted, make regular repayments and buy a diversified quality share portfolio.

Case study: margin loan

Masato is keen to build a share portfolio. He has $30 000 to invest. To increase his chances of making even more money he decides to borrow $70 000 from a financial institution that offer margin loans (for instance, Macquarie Equities). He will now have $100 000 to buy a quality diversified share portfolio. If his shares surge 25 per cent in value he will make a $25 000 capital gain. On the other hand, if his share portfolio plunges 25 per cent from $100 000 to $75 000, he will incur a $25 000 loss. To add salt to the wound he will be up for a margin call to restore the LVR. If he can't come up with the necessary funds within 24 hours his share portfolio will be sold.

Collapse of Storm Financial

Many investors were encouraged to mortgage their homes and take out margin loans to invest in Storm Financial investment-related products. When the Queensland-based managed fund collapsed in 2009 (as a consequence of the stock market plunging), many investors suffered substantial losses, and many were forced to sell their homes. This highlights the need to be fully aware of the nature of the investment products on offer, the risks of entering into complex margin loan arrangements, and whether they're suitable for your particular circumstances.

Watch your money grow: building wealth

There are many factors you'll need to compare and contrast when putting together a suitable investment portfolio to help you build up your wealth. An ideal investment is one that can deliver regular income and capital growth. Each asset class will have certain features that may or may not appeal to you. The tricky bit is trying to understand what you're doing and to separate the wheat from the chaff. In part II we examine the pros and cons of choosing specific investments and the various taxation issues you'll need to consider.

Chapter 5

Investing your hard-earned dough

Wealth creation commences from the moment you put your first dollar into a savings account. The great news here is you'll receive regular interest payments. Interest is cash you receive in return for the use of your money. There are many ways you can derive interest: the most common are savings accounts, cash management accounts and term deposits. Although this form of investing is considered to be relatively safe, if you persist with this policy you could soon find yourself going one step forward and two steps backwards. In this chapter I chat about the various ways you can derive interest.

What's on the list: interest securities

At one of my wealth creation talks I noticed a 91-year-old gentleman and his wife were in the audience. His wife asked me whether I could knock some sense into the old man, as all he wanted to do was keep his money in the bank and receive interest. 'Madam,' I quickly replied, 'at his age he can do whatever he wants!' In chapter 2 I indicated that to work out how much you should put into fixed interest you should subtract your age from 100. In this case I think the elderly gentleman may have just about got it right!

If you like investments that pay interest you will normally deposit money with reputable organisations such as banks, building societies and major corporations. In return for depositing money with them, you'll generally receive a fixed rate of interest (for example, 6 per cent per annum). The interest is normally credited to your account on a monthly, quarterly, half-yearly or yearly basis. And when the loan matures you would be expecting to get back the amount you originally invested. There are many different types of investments currently on the market that pay interest. The main ones you're likely to come across are listed here:

$ *Debentures.* These are medium- to long-term unsecured interest-bearing securities issued by reputable companies that need to raise finance. Debentures pay a fixed rate of interest during the term of the loan. In the event of the borrower defaulting, debenture holders rank higher than shareholders with respect to getting their money back.

$ *Term deposits.* A savings account with a bank that pays a fixed rate of interest for a specific period of time (for instance, 12 months). Financial penalties may apply if funds are withdrawn before the maturity date. This could become a bit of a nuisance if you lock your money away for a long period and you need to access those funds immediately.

$ *Cash management accounts.* A bank account that pays you interest at the end of each month and allows you to make regular deposits and cheque withdrawals.

$ *Bank bills.* This is a short-term investment with a bank (normally between 30 to 180 days) that you purchase at a discount to its face value. When the investment matures you will be paid its face value. For example, you pay $98 000 now for a bank bill with a face value of $100 000 payable on maturity. The return on your investment (interest) is the difference between the purchase price and face value (in this example $2000). The minimum you can invest is normally $100 000.

$ *Savings accounts.* A bank account that pays interest at regular intervals on money deposited. The investor can make regular deposits and withdrawals.

$ *Unsecured notes.* This is an unsecured high-risk investment normally issued by finance companies that pay a high rate of interest during the term of the loan. It's unsecured because the investor has no specific claims over the company's assets.

$ *Bonds.* These are interest-bearing securities normally issued by the government when they need to raise finance. Bonds pay a fixed rate of interest during the term of the loan. When the bond matures the holder will get back the face value (the amount initially invested). Bonds can be bought and sold on the Australian Securities Exchange before they mature.

Deriving interest

If everything goes according to plan, one of the great things about these types of investments is you'll receive regular income and your capital back on maturity. This means you can sleep well at night knowing that your capital will not decrease in value (as could be the case if you invest in shares and real estate). It's also a good short-term strategy that allows you to park your money for the time being and get some interest along the way. For example, during the 2008–09 global financial crisis if your money was safely tucked away in a term deposit earning interest, you would have been laughing all the way to the bank. Besides protecting your capital you would have been in an excellent position to buy quality blue chip shares at bargain-basement prices!

> **Handy tip**
>
> When interest rates are low (for example, 4 per cent), you should look at short-term investments; and when interest rates are high (for example, 8 per cent), the longer the term the better.

The magic of compound interest

Another major attraction with these investments is the magic of compound interest, where you can elect to reinvest the interest you derive and earn interest on your interest. For example, you deposit $10 000 for 10 years in a term deposit and the interest rate is 7 per cent compounding annually. When the loan matures your initial $10 000 deposit will grow to $19 671 (see table 5.1). And if the interest payments were more frequent (for example, payable every six months), the growth rate would be even higher. Although this might sound like a great way of building wealth, along the way you'll have to make provision for the payment of tax on the interest you derive each year. I often come across investment books that love telling you all about compound interest, but fail to advise you of the tax issues you'll need to consider. (For more details see ATO interpretive decision ID 2002/886 *Accessibility of compound interest* — available on the ATO website.)

Table 5.1: the amount of interest on $10 000 for 10 years

Year	Interest	Balance
1	$700	$10 700
2	$749	$11 449
3	$801.43	$12 250.43
4	$857.53	$13 107.96
5	$917.55	$14 025.51
6	$981.78	$15 007.30
7	$1 050.51	$16 057.81
8	$1 124.04	$17 181.86
9	$1 202.73	$18 384.59
10	$1 286.92	$19 671.51

Investing in government bonds: 'my word is my bond'

When federal and state governments need to raise capital to fund projects they issue government bonds. Bonds are interest-bearing securities that normally offer a fixed rate of interest (for example, 7 per cent) during the term of the bond (for example, 10 years). Each year you will be paid interest, and when the bond matures, the holder will get back the amount that was initially invested or 'face value' (for example, $10 000). Besides getting regular interest payments, bonds can be quickly bought and sold on the Australian Securities Exchange before they mature. The amount you'll pay or receive will depend on prevailing interest rates. For example, when interest rates rise (for example, from 7 per cent to 9 per cent), the value of your bond will fall (for example, from $10 000 to $8000) to compensate potential buyers locking into a lower rate. When this happens you will incur a loss on sale (in this case $2000). On the other hand, when interest rates fall (for example, from 7 per cent to 5 per cent), the value of your bond will increase (for example, from $10 000 to $12 000) as potential investors will pay you a premium to lock into the higher rate. In this case you stand to make a profit on sale.

Limitations and risks

We've all heard the old saying 'cash is king'. Although your money may be safe sitting in a term deposit earning interest, the risk if you persist with this policy is you could quickly find yourself going backwards. There are three major limitations (risks) that could have an adverse impact on your pursuit to build up your wealth:

$ *Interest rates can fall.* Investing in interest-bearing securities may be fine when interest rates are high (for instance, 10 per cent). As a rule of thumb the higher the rate the longer you should invest. But there's also a risk that interest rates could fall (for instance, to 3 per cent). This could turn into a major disaster if you're relying on the interest payments as your principal source of income. It goes without saying if interest rates fall significantly your cash flow will fall and your standard of living could be compromised. To add salt to the wound your interest payments are still liable to income tax, which means your net return will be even less.

$ *No capital growth.* A major drawback with this investment is if you continue investing in interest-bearing securities, you could find yourself going backwards in the long term. Although your capital may be safe it will not grow, and the purchasing power of your capital will start to diminish because of inflation. For example, if you invest $10 000 for five years in a term deposit you'll still have $10 000 when the loan matures. Might sound great. But the bad news here is you will not be able to buy the same amount of goods and services that you could have purchased five years earlier, and your capital will indirectly fall in value.

$ *Loss of opportunity.* During periods when alternate investments (particularly shares) are rocketing upwards, you could miss the boat if you decide to stick with term deposits. If you change your mind at a later date and switch strategies you will be paying more for investment assets that you could have purchased at a cheaper price.

Handy tip

In 2009 the federal government announced plans to issue inflation-linked bonds where interest payments will be adjusted in line with quarterly changes to the consumer price index. This is the index that's used to measure the rate of inflation in Australia. At the time of writing no further details had been released.

Taxing your interest payments

Under Australian tax law you're generally liable to pay tax when the interest is credited to your investment account. If you don't supply your tax file number (TFN) to an Australian financial institution at the time you open your account, it may withhold 46.5 per cent tax on the amount of interest that's credited to your account. This is referred to as 'TFN amounts deducted on interest'. The financial institution will tell you whether it did this. Any tax withheld will be taken into account when calculating your tax liability at the end of the financial year, and is refunded if you pay too much tax. Further, if you derive a substantial amount of interest you may need to prepare an 'Instalment Activity Statement' disclosing the interest you receive and pay tax on an ongoing basis (usually quarterly). The Australian Taxation Office will notify you if you need to do this. To meet your legal obligations you'll need to keep track of your interest payments. The tax you pay is credited against your end of financial year assessment.

Case study: interest versus dividends

Robert has $50 000 to invest. His marginal rate of tax is 30 per cent. He can either put his money in a term deposit paying 6 per cent interest ($3000) or buy shares. The dividend yield is

Case study *(cont'd)*: interest versus dividends

5 per cent fully franked ($2500). At first glance you would assume the term deposit offers the better return on his investment. But when you take tax into account you'll find the return on the shares is the better option. This is because you are not comparing apples with apples. The 6 per cent interest rate is a *pre-tax rate*, while the 5 per cent dividend yield paying fully franked dividends is an *after tax rate*. When you add the franking credit ($1071) to the dividend payment ($2500) the pre-tax or grossed-up dividend yield is actually 7.14 per cent (dividend $2500 + franking credit $1071 = $3571 ÷ capital invested $50 000 × 100 = 7.14 per cent). For more details see chapters 9 and 11.

Term deposit

Return on term deposit (6%)	$3000
Less tax payable	$900
Net return	$2100

Shares

Return on dividends (5%)	$2500
Franking credit	$1071
Less tax payable	$1071
Net return	$2500

If Robert pays no tax, the return on his shares will become even more attractive. This is because the franking credit ($1071) is refunded back to him, and he will receive $3571 ($2500 + $1071) rather than $3000 interest on his term deposit. So when all the smoke and mirrors are removed the five per cent dividend yield (fully franked) will give you a better return. Incidentally, no tax is payable if your taxable income is less than $16 000 (per 2010–11 tax rates).

Handy tip

As part of the Australian Taxation Office's ongoing compliance program, it regularly matches interest paid by Australia's major financial institutions against individual tax returns. So if you don't want to cop a stiff penalty make sure you disclose the correct amount of interest you receive each year in your individual tax return.

Starting a First Home Saver Account

To help individuals save for a deposit to buy or build their first home the federal government has introduced First Home Saver Accounts. Under this scheme the government will make a contribution to this account if a first home buyer makes an after-tax contribution of up to $5000 (indexed) into this account each year. For example, if you put $5000 into this account, the government will contribute a maximum of $850 (being 17 per cent of the amount you deposited). The great news here is the interest credited is taxed at the rate of 15 per cent, and any withdrawal you make to buy or build your first home is tax-free. However, the bad news (if you no longer wish to buy or build your first home) is you cannot withdraw your money. The balance is transferred to your superannuation fund and you may be liable to pay penalties for not using the funds to buy or build your first home. For more information on First Home Saver Accounts see <www.homesaver.treasury.gov.au>.

Handy tip

As a general rule there are no CGT issues to worry about when you invest in interest-bearing securities. This is because cash can't increase in value. Further, no GST is levied on financial transactions as money transactions are input taxed.

Chapter 6

Pooling your money: managed funds

If you're looking for someone to manage your money for you, look no further. Investing in managed funds may be the way to go. By the way, all the major Australian superannuation funds are managed funds. Under this investment arrangement you will be relying on financial experts to grow your wealth and pay you a regular income flow. In return, you will have to pay them a fee for managing your money. In this chapter I chat about the pros and cons of investing in managed funds and managed investment schemes.

Leaving it to the experts

Managed funds are mutual (or pooled) investment funds managed by Australia's leading financial institutions (such as banks and insurance companies). They give individual investors the opportunity to invest in a wide range of domestic and foreign investment portfolios. The investment strategy you'll select will depend on whether you're seeking income and/or capital growth. The great thing here is you can select an appropriate investment portfolio mix to suit your risk profile and objectives. The investment options (asset classes) include:

$ *cash:* such as bank bills, short-term deposits and government bonds (see chapter 5)

$ *balanced:* a mix of shares, fixed-interest securities and property

$ *growth:* where your money is predominantly invested in shares and property

$ *equity growth:* where your money is invested predominantly in Australian and international listed companies

$ *property:* where your money is invested predominantly in property

$ *foreign:* where your money is invested in international markets (for instance, US, Europe and Asia)

$ *indexed:* where your money is invested in a particular index (for instance, the S&P 200 index consisting of the top 200 companies listed on the ASX).

You may be given the opportunity to switch investment options, usually once a year free of charge. But you could be up for investment switching fees if you decide to do this more frequently. You should check the managed fund's policy regarding this matter.

If you want to invest in a managed fund you'll need to contact the financial institution directly. You will be required to fill out an application form attached to the product disclosure statement. This document will set out all the relevant information about the fund's investment products, the benefits and risks, and the fees you'll be charged. So it's important that you read this document prior to filling out the application form. The minimum you can invest is normally between $1000 and $5000 and you can make additional contributions as you become more affluent. Once you join you will be issued with units. The value of your units is market-linked. This means they will rise and fall in line with the prevailing market. Managed funds are ideal if you're an inexperienced investor or you would prefer someone to manage your investments for you. The great bit about this arrangement is you'll have professional fund managers looking after your investment portfolio, and you will receive regular fund statements regarding your investment holdings. Managed funds normally distribute income every six months, and you could make a capital gain if your units appreciate in value. Investing in managed funds is normally considered to be a long-term investment strategy (for instance, three to five years). So you may need to keep your units for a number of years before you're likely to see any capital appreciation.

The fees you had to have

Unfortunately, the bad news is you're liable to pay fees (and commissions) for the privilege of someone else managing your money. These fees are normally linked to the amount of funds you have under management. So it's important that you check out the various costs you're likely to be charged and how they're calculated. Remember, you're liable to pay these fees whether the fund is making money or losing money. It can be very upsetting if you find yourself paying a truckload of fees and your investments are going backwards. (During one of my wealth creation courses a disgruntled participant who wasn't impressed with the fees he was charged remarked, 'Why should I pay someone to lose my money when I can do it myself!') The types of fees you're likely to incur can include:

$ entry and exit fees in respect to establishing and terminating your fund

$ administration fees to cover general administration costs

$ management fees for managing your investment portfolio

$ external management costs paid to external investment managers and consultants

$ investment switching fees for changing investment options

$ transaction costs for buying and selling investment assets

$ performance fees for exceeding specified benchmarks.

The degree of success is predominantly dependent on the skill of the fund manager in choosing the right investment mix and picking the best time to buy and sell their respective investment portfolios. A major risk with this investment vehicle is the return on your investment may not be as high as owning specific investments outright. And you could lose money if your units decrease in value.

When you want to withdraw any funds you'll need to contact the financial institution directly and you'll normally get your money back within seven days. If you withdraw all your funds the amount you'll receive will depend on the market value of your units on the day they're sold. There's a possibility that you could incur exit fees when you close your account.

> **Handy tip**
>
> If you find the rate of return over the past five to 10 years is impressive, it doesn't imply that this will continue into the future. Remember, future performance is really measured from the moment you start investing your money with them. Keep in mind the old investment adage, 'past performance does not guarantee you future results'.

Bernard Madoff — Ponzi scheme

In 2009 investment manager Bernard Madoff was given a 150-year jail sentence for having committed the biggest investment fraud in US history, having lost over $50 billion of investor funds. For many years Madoff ran a 'Ponzi scheme' where he used newly deposited funds from investors to pay very attractive returns to investors who had previously deposited money with him. Unfortunately, many investors had placed undue trust that Madoff was doing everything by the book. He was predominantly relying on a steady flow of new deposits to meet earlier investment commitments rather than using the fund's earnings to do this. So as long as there were more deposits than withdrawals the investment arrangement would continue to flourish. The scheme subsequently collapsed in 2009 as a result of the global financial crisis, when there were more withdrawals than deposits.

Checklist: the pros and cons of managed funds

The following checklist provides a summary of the benefits and limitations in respect to investing in managed funds.

Benefits:

$ Your money is managed by highly qualified professional fund managers.

$ You'll be given a wide selection of asset classes to suit your personal circumstances and risk profile.

$ You'll receive income, which is normally payable twice a year.

$ There is a potential for capital growth if your units increase in value.

$ You can make regular contributions.

Limitations:

$ You're no longer in control of your money.

$ You will incur ongoing fees and charges.

$ The rate of return is uncertain.

$ Your capital is not guaranteed: there is a risk you could lose money.

If you want to know more about managed funds visit the Australian Securities & Investments Commission website <www.fido.asic.gov.au> and go to 'About financial products' then 'Managed funds'.

Managed investment schemes

Managed investment schemes give you the opportunity to invest in specific types of investment projects or schemes. The common ones are:

$ forestry managed investment schemes (tree plantations)

$ major infrastructure projects (toll roads, airports, water and sewage)

$ private equity funds (such as new inventions and medical research)

$ hedge funds (high-risk privately managed funds that invest in aggressive investment strategies such as short selling, derivatives and commodities).

A major problem with these types of investment opportunities is coming to terms with their business models and understanding their respective investment strategies. Before you can invest there is some legal paperwork you'll need to get hold off first. Under Australian company law you'll need to read the prospectus and/or product disclosure statement that licensed promoters must prepare when seeking funds. It will set out facts such as the investment arrangement's features, the benefits and risks, and any fees, commissions and charges you're likely to incur. The risk here is you may need to wait many years before you're likely to see any return on your money. In the meantime, while you're waiting your initial investment could fall in value, and you could be up for ongoing charges. So it's prudent that you check out stuff like your legal rights if something goes wrong and whether there's an established market if you want to get out early. Remember, if there's no market you could find yourself holding an investment that can't be readily converted into cash. And of course there's a further risk you could get back substantially less than what you originally put in. If you're keen to invest it may be a wise move to seek advice from a qualified professional such as a licensed financial planner (see chapter 1).

If you want to know more about investment schemes visit the Australian Securities & Investments Commission website <www.fido.asic.gov.au> and read 'Companies and investment schemes' under 'Publications & resources'.

Collapse of forestry managed investment schemes

In chapter 2 it was pointed out you should avoid making investment decisions solely to gain a tax benefit. And to this we can add if you don't fully understand what you're doing, why bother investing. There's an old investment adage that states, 'build on what you know; don't buy what you don't understand'. Unfortunately, many investors who were encouraged to invest in forestry managed investment schemes to gain an upfront tax deduction would have lost a packet following the collapse of Timbercorp and Great Southern in 2009.

> **Handy tip**
>
> For a comprehensive discussion on the taxation of forestry managed investment schemes the Australian Taxation Office has issued a fact sheet titled *Forestry managed investment schemes.* You can get a copy from the Tax Office website ‹www.ato.gov.au›.

Property trusts

Property trusts are managed funds that invest predominantly in major residential and commercial property developments located throughout Australia (for instance, residential accommodation, office space, industrial, rural and large shopping centres). So if you want some exposure in the property market and don't want to outlay a truckload of money, investing in property trusts may be the way to go. This could appeal to investors who wish to maintain a diversified investment portfolio (especially investors who run a self managed superannuation fund). As is the case with other categories of managed funds you will be issued with units. The value of your units will rise and fall in line with the prevailing property market. Property trusts normally enter into long-term leases and pay regular income (the yield is generally around six to eight per cent per annum), and you can make money if your units increase in value. You can also lose money if property valuations fall. Many of the leading property trusts are listed on the ASX. This will allow you to buy and sell your units quickly, as is the case with shares. Property trusts listed in the S&P/ASX 200 index include:

$ Bunnings Warehouse Property Trusts (BWP)

$ CFS Retail Property Trust (CFX)

$ Commonwealth Property Office Fund (CPA)

$ Goodman Group (GMG)

$ GPT Group (GPT)

$ ING Industrial Fund (IIF)

$ Macquarie Countrywide Trust (MCW)

$ Mirvac Group (MGR)

$ Stockland (SGP)

$ Westfield Group (WDC).

Handy tip

If you intend to use borrowed money to invest in a property trust, some of your interest payments may not be tax deductible. For more information read Taxation Ruling IT 2684 *Deductibility of interest on money borrowed to acquire units in a property unit trust.* You can get a copy from the Tax Office website.

When assessing which property trust to invest money with you'll need to consider issues such as:

$ the different types of property they hold (for instance residential, commercial, rural)

$ how current economic conditions could affect property valuations and returns

$ who the tenants are (for instance, federal and state government departments)

$ when property leases are due to expire; the longer the lease the better the situation

$ how much income the property trust derives each year

$ their policy regarding assessable distributions and non-assessable distributions (see figure 6.1, overleaf)

$ the ongoing fees and charges you're likely to incur.

Figure 6.1: property trust distributions

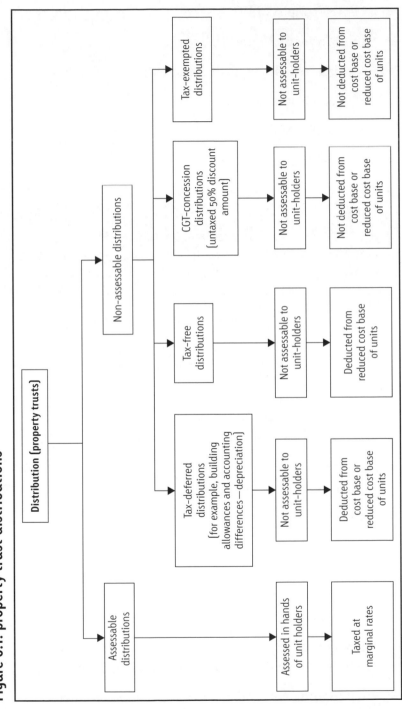

Getting a property trust distribution

As shown in figure 6.1, property trusts normally make two types of distributions, namely assessable distributions such as rental receipts, and non-assessable distributions, particularly:

⇒   *tax-deferred distributions.* Not assessable to unit holders. Under CGT provisions they are deducted from the unit's cost base or reduced cost base.

⇒   *tax-free distributions.* Not assessable to unit holders. They are deducted from the unit's reduced cost base when calculating a capital loss.

⇒   *CGT-concession distributions.* Not assessable to unit holders and not deducted from the unit's cost base or reduced cost base.

⇒   *tax-exempted distributions.* Not assessable to unit holders and not deducted from the cost base or reduced cost base.

Chapter 7

Making money on the sharemarket

As share prices can fluctuate daily the anxiety that you could lose money is a constant feeling you may experience. Sure you can drop a bundle if share prices plunge. But you can also make heaps if they rise. Provided you do your homework and invest sensibly, owning shares can be a very rewarding and lucrative way of building up your wealth. In this chapter I chat about the basics, and explain that investing in the sharemarket is not all doom and gloom. I also chat about the different ways you can invest in shares.

To gain confidence dealing with this type of wealth-creating asset, it's important that you understand the fundamentals—both good and bad. The following information explains the nuts and bolts of investing in the sharemarket.

Cashing in your chips: highly liquid

During one of my sharemarket courses a woman casually said to me, 'I own a $50 000 share portfolio but I have no cash that I can quickly access'. When the first aid officer helped me recover from the sudden shock of hearing such a statement, I had to remind her that shares are effectively a substitute for cash. In chapter 8 I emphasise it normally takes no more than a few seconds to buy and sell them (especially if it's done online). And you'll normally get your money back within a few days. Alternative investments like managed investment schemes, real estate and collectables could take an eternity to sell. So what does all this mean? Shares allow you to quickly get in and out at minimal cost. And you'll be able to take advantage of any good buying opportunities in other asset classes that may pop up from time to time.

Shares also give you the opportunity to sell small parcels at short notice. For example, you own 1000 BHP Billiton shares and you need to sell 500 shares to access some cash quickly. Unfortunately, you can't do this with alternative investments such as real estate and collectables: you can't rock up to an auctioneer and try to sell your front bedroom or the left-hand corner of an expensive painting by a famous artist! Although there is no minimum number of shares you can sell, the brokerages fees payable to sell minute parcels could make the transaction uneconomical.

Adding to the pile: investing small amounts

One of the great things about shares is you don't need a truckload of money to start the ball rolling (as is the case with wealth creation assets like real estate). There are simply no set minimums. With as little as $1000 you can start a small share portfolio and build from there. And you can buy more shares as you become more affluent. Further, when you become a shareholder, you may be given the opportunity to participate in rights issues and dividend reinvestment plans, where you can buy more shares direct from the company. These offers to buy additional shares are normally at a discount to the current market price, and no brokerage fees are payable! A great example that comes to mind is the National Australia Bank share purchase plan. In August 2009 shareholders were given the opportunity to buy shares direct from the company at $21.50 per share. When the shares were allotted to the shareholders a few weeks later, they were trading at around the $28 mark (you little ripper!).

Counting your money: prices published daily

I love counting my money, especially when share prices are rising. The great thing about owning shares is you can instantly check their current market value, while sitting in front of your laptop sipping a cool drink at a popular holiday resort. If they go up in value you can quickly sell them and take a profit, and either buy them back again if they fall in value or move into something else. For example, on Monday you pay $30 for 1000 shares. On Tuesday at 10.05 am they jump to $31.25. You immediately sell them and pocket a lazy $1250 profit (less brokerage; building wealth and loving it!). At 2.45 pm they fall back to $30. So you decide to buy the shares back. Unfortunately, you can't do this with alternative wealth-creating assets like real estate. Although you can get a sworn valuation it's meaningless unless you can find a buyer who's willing to pay the price you're asking.

Rolling in dough: receiving a dividend

The major Australian companies listed on the ASX normally declare two dividends around the same time each year. They are called an interim (or mid-year) dividend and a final dividend. If you have a number of companies that declare dividends on different dates, it's possible to get a steady and reliable income flow. For example, CBA normally pays dividends in March and October while NAB pays dividends in July and December. If you also have Telstra in your portfolio, which normally pays dividends in April and September, you're on the way to getting a nice little income flow going.

It's also possible for you to qualify for a dividend within a few days of buying your shares. When a company declares a dividend it will announce the ex-dividend date. This means if you buy the shares before the ex-dividend date you will qualify for the dividend. For example on 1 February the company declares 50 cents per share dividend and announces the ex-dividend date is 14 February. If you buy the shares before 14 February you'll qualify for the 50 cents per share dividend when they're paid. If you do this you'll be buying the shares cum-dividend (meaning with the dividend attached). But the good news gets even better: if you sell them after they go ex-dividend (for instance on 16 February), you'll still get the dividend even though you no longer own the shares! The person who buys them from you misses out. Contrast this with a term deposit where you may need to wait six months before interest is credited to your account. Unfortunately, when a company goes ex-dividend you may find the share price falls. This is because the company has now got an obligation to pay a dividend. So you may need to take this into account if you plan to sell your shares in the short term. Besides getting a dividend, you'll also receive a franking credit if the dividend is franked. In chapter 9 I point out that franking credits are tax offsets that you can apply against the net tax payable on the dividend (and other income) you derive.

Handy tip

If you buy shares just before they go ex-dividend (and assuming the company declares a dividend every six months), you could qualify for three dividend payments within 13 months of buying them!

Making easy money: capital growth

One of the great things about investing in the sharemarket is shares have the capacity to increase in value—sometimes very quickly. You'll generally find share price growth is primarily dependent on a company's ability to grow its business and make more profits. So it's important that you invest your money wisely (see chapter 10). The more profits a company can generate the greater the chance that your wealth will grow in the long term. It's as simple as that! In the meantime, no tax is payable on any 'unrealised gains' until the shares are sold. And if you hold them for more than 12 months the added bonus here is only 50 per cent of the gain you make on sale is liable to tax (see chapter 9).

Rights issue

When companies need to raise additional capital they will give you the right to buy additional shares at below their current market price. For example, when Blue Scope Steel needed additional capital they offered their shareholders in May 2009 the right to buy more shares at $1.55 per share. When they made this announcement the shares were trading at around the $2.50 mark. Investors who exercised their right to buy them would have picked up a bargain. When the shares were trading above $3 a few months later they would have doubled their money!

No annoying charges: no holding costs

The great news about owning a share portfolio is there are no ongoing costs (see chapter 2). Unfortunately, you can't say this when you buy a property or put money into a managed fund. For example, if you own a property you will incur ongoing costs like land tax, rates, insurance and repairs (which could amount to a substantial sum). And if you choose to invest in a managed fund you will have to pay them umpteen ongoing fees and charges for the privilege of managing your money (see chapter 6). Speaking from personal experience, it's exhilarating to come home each night and not find any annoying bills relating to my share portfolio in my 'in tray'!

The risks you need to take

The benefits you can gain from investing in the sharemarket may sound great. But the trade-off here is the risks you'll need to take to gain them. There are three major concerns that you'll need to consider before you invest in the share market.

$ *Share valuations could fall.* Although share prices can rise in value, they can fall just as quickly. There's a stock market adage that goes along the lines of 'the market hates uncertainty'. Put simply, share prices are very sensitive to global events and downgrades in company-earning forecasts. So if your share portfolio were to take a nosedive you could suffer a substantial loss if you sell them. By the way, if you find yourself in this situation keep in mind an old adage that you should 'never hold on to a loser just to collect the dividends'. To reduce the risk of losing money it's prudent that you invest in many quality blue chip companies from different sectors of the Australian economy (for instance, companies in the S&P/ASX 20 index, see table 10.1 in chapter 10, on pages 138–139). But let's end on a positive note: you can now buy these shares at a cheaper price!

$ *Dividends could fall or cease.* The payment of a dividend is at the discretion of the company directors. Shareholders have no right to demand a payment or determine the amount they should receive. During the 2008–09 global financial crisis, many companies listed on the ASX stopped paying dividends to shareholders or reduced the amount they normally declare. This could have an adverse impact on your standard of living if you're relying on these dividends to help fund your lifestyle.

$ *Companies could cease trading.* There is always a risk a company could fall into financial difficulty and cease trading. One classic example is the collapse of US merchant bank Lehman Brothers in September 2008 (see chapter 2). If this happens there's a risk your shares could become worthless. Again, it pays to invest in a number of companies. Incidentally, under the CGT provisions, when company shares become worthless you can claim a capital loss. The capital loss can be deducted from a current or future capital gain (see chapter 9). So as they say in the classics, all is not lost!

Handy tip

To reduce your exposure to potential losses you could consider applying a 'stop-loss' strategy. If you adopt this plan of attack you will sell your shares if they fall to a predetermined price. For example, you pay $10 for shares in Crabtree Ltd. If they fall, say, 15 per cent from $10 to $8.50 you will immediately sell them. If you do this you will limit your loss to no more than 15 per cent and you'll protect your capital from falling further in value.

Bear market: don't feed the bears

Technically, a bear market is said to occur when the sharemarket falls more than 20 per cent in less than 12 months from its recorded peak. This happened in Australia when the S&P/ASX 200 index fell more than 20 per cent in January 2008 from a peak of 6853.6 points on 1 November 2007. In November 2008 the index had fallen below 3700 points.

Fannie Mae and Freddie Mac

During the 2008 global financial crisis (where share prices were plunging from every direction), two major US mortgage finance companies, 'Fannie Mae' and 'Freddie Mac', got into financial difficulty as a consequence of the subprime mortgage crisis. To stop them from collapsing the US government was forced to take them over. Otherwise, it would have caused a chain reaction with other local and global financial institutions becoming vulnerable to collapsing. Stock markets throughout the world would have plunged even further, which would have had an adverse impact on everyone's personal wealth.

Investing in derivatives

There is an alternative way you can invest in the sharemarket other than to buy the shares outright. Another method is to invest in derivatives. A derivative is defined as a financial instrument that derives its value from the value of the underlying investment (such as shares). Incidentally, the first thing that'll hit you when you examine derivates is they have their own unique language. The three most common ways of investing in derivatives are listed here (see also figure 7.1):

$ exchange-traded options (ETO)

$ warrants

$ contracts for difference (CFD).

Handy tip

It's possible for you to speculate in the price movements of foreign currencies (commonly known as FOREX). There are numerous websites that explain how this way of investing works, for example, ‹www.forextrading.com›.

Figure 7.1 derivatives

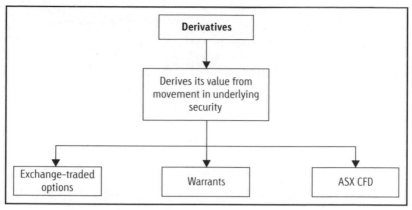

Exchange-traded options

One popular way to buy and sell shares is to invest in call and put options that are listed on the ASX. These options are known as exchange-traded options (ETO). They give investors the opportunity to buy and sell shares at a specified price (exercise price) on or before a specified date in the future (expiry date). These types of options are not issued by companies but are listed on the ASX. There are currently over 50 ETO stocks that you can trade on the ASX. You can get a detailed list from the ASX website <www.asx.com.au>. If you want to buy a call or put option you will need to pay a premium. Under this arrangement the person who receives the premium bears all the risk. This is because that person (known as the option writer) must either buy or sell the shares at the specified price. The size of each contract is 1000 shares. If you don't exercise your right to buy or sell the shares by the expiry date, your option will expire worthless—and the option writer will pocket the premium. In the meantime, these options can be traded on the ASX before they expire. Exchange-traded options can also be used to hedge (protect) your current position in a volatile market (for example, you can buy a put option to protect your shares if they fall in value).

Checklist: characteristics of call and put options

$ You can hedge (protect) your share portfolio against adverse share price movements.

$ For a small outlay you can lock into a predetermined buy or sell price now and wait to see what could happen before the option expires.

$ Your risk is limited to the premium you pay.

$ If you're the option writer the risk is unlimited but you get to keep the premium (see case study: selling a call option, following).

$ Like shares, options can be quickly bought and sold on the ASX.

$ Options do not give you the right to receive a dividend.

$ The potential profit is unlimited if the price of the underlying shares moves in your direction. For example, you exercise your right to buy the shares at $10 and the current market price is $15.

$ For a small outlay you can speculate on a large volume of shares.

Handy tip

The ASX Derivatives Division has issued two publications titled *Understanding Options Trading* and *Understanding Options Strategies* that provide comprehensive details about investing in options. You can get a free copy from the ASX or from its website ‹www.asx.com.au›.

Buying a call option

Buying a call option gives the buyer the right (but not the obligation) to buy a specified number of shares (for instance,

1000 CBA shares) on or before the expiry date. You will need to pay a premium to the seller (the option writer) for the right to buy those shares at the exercise price. If you don't exercise your right to buy by the expiry date the option becomes worthless. The most you'll lose is the premium you paid. Incidentally, you can sell your call option on the ASX before it expires. Buying a call option is worth doing if you think a particular company's share price is likely to rise between the date you buy the call option and the date the option expires.

Case study: buying a call option

On 1 October you pay a $1 premium (the cost of the option) for the right but not obligation to buy a CBA share for $40 on or before 30 November (the date the call option expires). If the market price of a CBA share on 1 October is $35 the option is currently 'out of the money'. If you buy this call option you'll be hoping CBA will be trading above $41.00 (purchase price plus the premium paid) on or before 30 November. If CBA surges to $50 you'll be 'in the money' as you can exercise your right to buy them at $40! Alternatively, if the market value of your call option is trading at $9 you can sell it on the ASX and make a profit on the option. But if CBA plunges to $30 you'll be 'out of the money' as it's unlikely you'll exercise your right to buy at $40. Under these circumstances the most you'll lose is the $1 premium you paid.

Case study: selling a call option

If you're the seller of the CBA call option you'll receive the $1 premium. But the risk here is you're obligated to sell the specified number of CBA shares at the exercise price of $40 on or before 30 November. So if CBA surges to $50 and the buyer exercises their right to buy them at $40 you must deliver (sell) the shares at that price. But if CBA plunges to $30 you get to keep the $1 premium, as it's unlikely the buyer will pay you $40 when the market price is $30. In the meantime this option can be sold on the ASX before the expiry date.

Buying a put option

A put option is the reverse of buying a call option. Buying a put option gives the buyer the right to sell a specified number of shares on or before a specified date in the future. If you want to do this you will need to pay a premium to the seller of a put option. Buying a put option is similar to buying insurance, as you will be effectively protecting yourself against a possible fall in the price of your shares. So if this was to occur, you can exercise your right to sell your shares at the specified price. Under this arrangement the most you'll lose is the premium you paid, and this will happen if the company's share price rises.

Case study: buying a put option

On 1 August the current market price of a NAB share is $40. As there is a chance they could fall in value you decide to buy a put option which will expire on 31 August. The premium for the right (but not obligation) to sell your NAB share at $40 on or before 31 August is $2. If you find two weeks later that your NAB shares had plunged to $30, you can exercise your right to sell them at $40 (minus the $2 premium you paid). On the other hand if NAB surges to $50, it's unlikely that you'll exercise your right to sell them at $40 given the market price is now $50. Under these circumstances, the most you'll lose is the $2 premium you paid.

Warrants

A warrant is an option to buy or sell the underlying security (shares) and is similar in nature to exchange-traded equity options. The key difference here is the transaction is between the purchaser and issuer of the warrant. Warrants are normally issued by the major Australian banks (for instance, CBA, WBC and Credit Suisse). As is the case with exchange-traded options, a warrant gives the purchaser the right but not the obligation to buy from the issuer or sell to the issuer the underlying shares (for example, Woolworths Ltd shares), at a predetermined price (referred to as the exercise price), on or before the date the warrant expires. The great bit about this arrangement is the most you can lose is the premium you pay. When you hold a warrant you can either buy the underlying shares if you exercise your right to buy them, or you can sell the warrant on the Australian Securities Exchange before it expires. Warrants are issued as either American-style warrants or European-style warrants. If you can exercise your right to buy (or sell) the warrant before the expiry date, the warrant is an 'American-style' warrant. But if you can only exercise your right to buy (or sell) on the expiry date, the warrant is a 'European-style' warrant. The information about a particular warrant is set out in a document called an Offering Circular, which you can get from the issuer. There are many different types of warrants that you can buy. The most popular ones are 'equity warrants' and 'instalment warrants'. Details of the various warrants currently on the market are published in newspapers and on the ASX website.

Checklist: characteristics of warrants

$ Warrants are similar to exchange-traded options.

$ The potential loss is limited to the premium you pay.

$ You are not ordinarily entitled to receive any dividends.

$ Warrants are issued as American style or European style.

$ Warrants are normally issued by major financial institutions such as banks.

$ Warrants can be quickly bought and sold on the ASX.

$ Settlement can be a cash payment or physical delivery of the shares.

Handy tip

The ASX Derivatives Division has issued a publication called *Warrants — Understanding trading and investment warrants* that provides details about investing in warrants. You can get a free copy from the ASX or from its website ‹www.asx.com.au›.

Case study: buying a call warrant

On 17 February 2010 you're keen to buy shares in Crabtree Ltd. The current market price is $5.61 per share. You check the newspaper (or your online broker) and you come across the following warrant:

⇛   Crabtree Ltd call warrant — issuer Macquarie Bank (MC) — American style

⇛   expiry date: 27 August 2010

⇛   exercise price: $6.10

⇛   sell: $0.26 cents

⇛   conversion ratio: 1:1 (meaning one warrant = one share).

If you buy one warrant for 26 cents you will have the right but not the obligation to buy one Crabtree Ltd share for $6.10 from Macquarie Bank. Because the warrant is 'American style' you can exercise your right to buy the underlying shares (Crabtree Ltd) on or before the expiry date (27 August 2010). This warrant is currently 'out of the money'. So on 17 February 2010 you decide to buy 20 000 warrants @ 26 cents — total outlay $5200. The premium to participate ($5200) is the most you can lose. On 9 August 2010 you find the market price of Crabtree Ltd is $8.15, and — guess what — you can buy them at $6.10 from the issuer (Macquarie Bank) if you exercise your right to buy. This warrant is now 'in the money' as you can buy the shares at below the market price. But there's more good news. In the meantime, you find the value of your warrant had increased from 26 cents to $2.08 (being the difference between the current market price ($8.15) and exercise price ($6.10) plus a further 3 cents because the warrant had

> not yet expired). You decide to sell your warrant on the ASX and receive $41600, giving you a profit of $36400 (less brokerage: ah, building wealth and loving it!) This is not a bad result in anyone's language, given the most you could lose is $5200 if Crabtree Ltd had not risen in value! If you find on the expiry date that Crabtree Ltd is trading at $5 you will not exercise your right to buy them at $6.10, given you can buy them on the open market at $5. Under these circumstances the most you'll lose is the premium you paid.

Contracts for difference: playing two-up

A contract for difference (CFD) is a derivative that allows you to speculate in the price movement of underlying securities (for instance, Woodside Petroleum) without actually owning them outright. A CFD transaction is a short-term contract (usually no more than a few days) between a buyer and CFD provider. The main CFD providers that deal with these financial instruments are:

$ CMC Markets

$ IG Markets

$ CommSec

$ MQ Prime

$ E*Trade Australia.

Under this arrangement both parties will take an opposite view as to whether the value of the underlying security (shares) will increase or decrease in value. It's similar to tossing a coin and betting on whether it will come up heads or tails. Settlement is by way of a cash payment, being the difference between the opening and closing value of the underling security. If the outcome is positive (that is, buyer rightly calls heads) the CFD provider pays the difference (the increase in value), and the buyer will make a quick profit. But what if the outcome is negative (buyer calls heads but comes down tails)? Under these circumstances the buyer pays the difference to the CFD provider and will incur a loss. To reduce the risk of losing money a buyer can take out a form of insurance (called a guaranteed stop-loss) to limit any potential losses that could arise.

If you enter into these transactions with a view to making a profit (which is normally the case), any profit you make is treated as taxable income and any loss you incur is a tax deductible expense. In the unlikely event that you can prove to the Tax Office the purpose of entering into the transaction was *not to make a profit*, the question now is, would you be taxed under the CGT provisions? Well, yes and no. Although a CFD is a CGT asset, the Tax Office takes the view that what you're basically doing is betting that the underlying security will either increase or decrease (merely playing two-up, in a manner of speaking). So, any gain or loss you make will be disregarded under the CGT gambling provisions. Great news if you make a capital gain, but an absolute tragedy if you make a capital loss (given the loss can't be claimed). If you find yourself in this dilemma you should seek professional advice.

Handy tip

The Australian Taxation Office's views on the tax treatment of financial contracts for differences are set out in Tax Ruling TR 2005/15 *Income tax — tax consequences of financial contracts for differences*. You can get a copy from the ATO website ‹www.ato.gov.au›.

Chapter 8

How to buy and sell shares

So you want to get into the sharemarket and you don't know what to do? Then you've come to the right place. In this chapter I show you the ropes and explain the steps you'll need to follow if you want to buy and sell shares on the Australian Securities Exchange (ASX).

Back to basics

In chapter 2 it was pointed out that when you invest in the sharemarket you'll be hoping that companies listed on the ASX will run successful businesses and make you lots of money. Under corporations law a company is a separate legal entity. This means it has an independent existence, can own assets and can run a business in its own name. A company can be either a private company or public company.

The Australian Securities Exchange gives publicly listed companies the opportunity to raise capital from the general public to fund their business operations. This is done through the issue of ordinary shares. It also gives investors the opportunity to buy and sell their shares in an orderly manner. This is commonly known as buying and selling shares on the secondary market. When you buy ordinary shares you will become a part owner or shareholder of that company. One important duty is to appoint company directors to manage the company's business activities. Ordinary shareholders have the right to attend and vote at the annual general meeting, and receive a share of any net profits the company makes—called dividends—and any return of capital. The more profitable a company becomes the more likely you'll receive a dividend and the greater the chance that your shares will increase in value.

Annual general meeting: raising an important issue

A woman who owned shares in a company that makes stationery products attended the annual general meeting. At the meeting each shareholder received a sample bag of the company's goods. When the lady found there was no diary among the stationery items she was outraged. During question time when complex business questions were raised and debated, the woman informed the CEO of the missing diary in her bag. The CEO informed her that the matter would be immediately attended to. The moral of the story is you've got to get your priorities right.

Handy tip

Share price growth is primarily dependent on a company's ability to continually grow its business base and increase its profits (or earnings per share).

Contacting a stockbroker

If you want to buy shares in a public company listed on the ASX you'll need to contact a stockbroker. This is a person who's authorised to buy and sell shares on the ASX. There are two types of stockbrokers that deal with shares: full-service brokers and discount (or online) brokers. Incidentally, you're protected under the 'national guarantee fund' if a stockbroker fails to follow proper procedures when buying and selling shares on your behalf. Full-service brokers can give you the deluxe treatment, which is great news if you're a beginner. For example, they can help you put together a share portfolio, give you their research material on specific companies, and take buy and sell orders. In return each time they do a share trade for you they'll charge you a brokerage fee. This can vary from between 0.5 per cent and 1.5 per cent of the purchase or sale price. In contrast, discount brokers (also known as online brokers) take buy and sell orders only. But the good news here is you can access all their research material free of charge on their respective websites (see table 8.1). They will even allow you to check the current price of every company listed on the ASX. The brokerage fees they charge are much lower than full-service brokers, normally around 0.4 per cent of the purchase or sale price.

Table 8.1: leading online brokers

Broker	Website
Bell Direct	‹www.belldirect.com.au›
Scottrade	‹www.scottrade.com›
CommSec	‹www.comsec.com.au›
Share Builder	‹www.sharebuilder.com›
E*Trade	‹www.etrade.com.au›
TD Ameritrade	‹www.tdameritrade.com›
Macquarie Edge	‹www.macquarie.com.au/edge›
Trade King	‹www.tradeking.com›
OptionsXpress	‹www.optionsxpresss.com›
Zecco Trading	‹www.zecco.com›

Before you can rock up and start buying and selling your shares you'll need to become either broker-sponsored under CHESS or sponsored by the company. Under CHESS (which stands for Clearing House Electronic Sub-register System) you'll need to sign a sponsorship agreement with your stockbroker before you can start trading with them. Once the paperwork has been completed you'll be issued with a Holder Identification Number (HIN). This number is used whenever you trade with that particular stockbroker. If you don't want to do business with them any more you can simply transfer your current shareholdings to another stockbroker. On the other hand, under the company sponsorship option, the company in which you purchase shares will issue you with their Security Registration Number (SNR). Under this option you're basically a free agent in that you're not tied to any particular stockbroker. This may sound great at first glance, but a major dilemma with this arrangement is you may experience difficulty selling your shares immediately. To overcome this minor irritation it may be more advantageous for you to become broker-sponsored under CHESS at the outset.

Handy tip

For more details about the stock market, stockbrokers and all the companies listed on the ASX visit the Australian Securities Exchange website ‹www.asx.com.au›.

Buying and selling your shares

So you've done your homework found a suitable stockbroker and you're itching to start making money. The following explains what happens when you buy and sell shares from a stockbroker.

Buying shares

When you contact your stockbroker by phone or via the internet to place an order to buy, the first thing that'll hit you is how little time it takes to do a trade. If you buy them 'at market' (being the current market price) it'll normally take no more than a few seconds to do the transaction (especially if it's done online). If you want to pay less than market price you'll have to wait and hope the share price will fall. But there's no guarantee that this will happen. Keep in mind Murphy's Law—when you want the shares to fall they'll probably go up and when you want them to rise they'll most likely go down! So it's important that you know exactly what you're doing as mistakes could cost you dearly.

Once your order to buy is executed your stockbroker will immediately issue a buy contract note (or invoice) setting out the full details of the transaction (see figure 8.1, overleaf). If you do this transaction online you'll normally receive the buy contract note as soon as the trade is completed. A hard copy is forwarded to you by mail within a couple of days and full payment is required within four days. So you'll need to have the necessary money to buy them or all hell will break loose if you fail to meet the deadline. To overcome this possibility it's recommended that you link your bank account details with your stockbroker's account. That way all funds can be instantaneously transferred from one account to the other.

> **Handy tip**
>
> Make sure you keep all your buy contract notes in a safe place, as these documents tell you the date you bought the shares and your purchase costs. You'll need to use this information to work out whether you've made a capital gain or capital loss for tax purposes (see case study: using your buy and sell contract notes, pages 116–117).

Figure 8.1: buy contract note

	BUY
	Contract Note
Stockbroker's Services Ltd	

Melissa Jones
100 Shares Avenue
Smithville WA

Tax Invoice

We have bought the following securities for you:
Company: Crabtree Ltd
Security: Ordinary Fully Paid

Date:	26 July 2010
Contract note number:	987654
Account number:	3211234
Total units:	1000
Cost price:	$5.60
Consideration (AUD):	$5600.00
Brokerage & costs including GST:	$100.00
Total cost:	$5700.00
Settlement date:	29 July 2010

A couple of weeks after you buy the shares the company will issue a 'Holding Statement' recording 'Quantity On' (see figure 8.2). By the way, when you examine this document you'll find it won't tell you the date you bought the shares and all your purchase costs. So you should keep the Holding Statement with the buy contract note you receive from your stockbroker.

Selling shares

The steps you'll need to take to sell your shares are similar to the way you buy them. When you decide to sell you'll need to contact your stockbroker again and place a sell order. If you sell 'at market' — current market price — a sale will normally happen very quickly. On the other hand, if you were to set a price that's above the current market price there's no guarantee you'll sell them at that price. For example, you find the current market price is $7.56 but you're hanging out for $7.75. If no buyers are prepared to pay this price it's unlikely that you'll sell them immediately. And there's a risk you may not get this price in the foreseeable future. In the meantime, while you're waiting, there's a risk the price of your shares could fall.

Figure 8.2: holding statement

CRABTREE LTD
Melissa Jones
100 Shares Avenue
Smithville WA

Holder Identification Number (HIN)
007123987654

Security class: ORDINARY FULLY PAID SHARES

Holding Statement as at 13 August 2010

Date:	13 August 2010
Transaction type:	Transfer
Opening balance:	0
Quantity on:	1000
Quantity off:	
Holding balance:	1000

At the time of sale you may need to quote your HIN or SNR number to your stockbroker to verify the number of shares you own in the company. As soon as your sell order is executed you'll be issued with a sell contract note (or invoice) setting out the full details of the sale transaction (see figure 8.3, overleaf), and you'll normally get your money back within a few days of selling them. About two weeks later the company will send you an amended 'Holding Statement' recording 'Quantity Off'. It's as simple as that!

Once the sale has been completed you'll need to figure out the amount of profit or loss you made on the sale. To do this quickly all you need to do is get the details from your buy and sell contract notes (see case study: using your buy and sell contract notes). Incidentally, I chat about the tax issues associated with making a capital gain (or loss) in chapter 9.

Figure 8.3: sell contract note

	SELL **Contract Note**

Stockbroker's Services Ltd

Melissa Jones
100 Shares Avenue
Smithville WA

Tax Invoice

We have sold the following securities for you
Company: Crabtree Ltd
Security: Ordinary Fully Paid

Date:	24 November 2010
Contract note number:	4790041
Account number:	3211234
Total units:	1000
Sale price:	$8.90
Consideration (AUD):	$8900.00
Brokerage & costs including GST:	$125.00
Net proceeds:	$8775
Settlement date:	27 November 2010

Case study: using your buy and sell contract notes

On 25 July 2010 Melissa Jones contacted her stockbroker and purchased 1000 Crabtree Ltd shares at $5.60 per share and she paid $100 brokerage fees and GST to buy them. According to the buy contract note she received the total amount payable was $5700 (see figure 8.1). On 24 November 2010 Melissa contacted her stockbroker and sold her 1000 Crabtree Ltd shares at $8.90 per share and she paid $125 brokerage fees and GST to sell them. According to the sell contract note the net proceeds on sale was $8775 (see figure 8.3).

Capital proceeds (sale price; figure 8.3)	$8900
Less:	
Purchase price (figure 8.1)	$5600
Purchase costs (figure 8.1)	$100
Sale costs (figure 8.3)	$125
	$5825
Net profit	**$3075**

As the shares were held for less than 12 months, Melissa made a non-discount capital gain (meaning the entire gain is liable to tax). For more details see chapter 9.

Chapter 9

Taxing your share transactions

If you own shares it's important that you know how your dividends are taxed and how to calculate a capital gain or capital loss when you sell them. You'll also need to know what expenses you can claim as a tax deduction. In this chapter I discuss the major taxation issues associated with owning shares.

Taxing your dividends

The great bit about being a shareholder is you get the right to receive a share of the company's profits, commonly known as dividends. The top companies listed on the ASX normally declare and pay two dividends each year, and you're generally liable to pay tax when they're paid to you. When a company pays a dividend it must tell its shareholders whether the dividend is fully franked, partially franked or unfranked. This information is included in the shareholder dividend statement you get when you receive a dividend (see figure 9.1). A franked dividend means the company has paid tax on the profits it makes, and when this happens you get a franking credit. Franking credits are tax offsets that you can apply against the net tax payable on the dividends (and other income) you derive. The great news here is if your total franking credits exceed the net tax payable the Australian Taxation Office refunds the balance, and the overall return on your investment will increase. For example, if a company pays you a $10 000 fully franked dividend you'll get $10 000 plus a $4285 franking credit (see figure 9.1). When you lodge your individual tax return you must include both amounts as part of your assessable income ($14 285). You're taxed on the 'grossed-up amount' ($14 285), and the franking credit ($4285) is applied against the net tax payable. On the other hand, if you get a dividend that's only partially franked (for instance, 50 per cent) the franking credit is reduced (for instance, from $4285 to $2143). But you'll get no franking credits if the dividend is unfranked and you're liable to pay tax on the full amount.

Figure 9.1: shareholder dividend statement

Shareholder Dividend Statement	
Fully Franked Interim Dividend Half-Year Ended 31 December 20XX	
Payment date	17 December 20XX
CRABTREE LIMITED	
Class of shares	Ordinary shares
Dividend rate per share	80 cents
Number of shares held	12 500
Franked amount	$10 000
Franking credit	$4285
Dividend amount	$10 000

While I'm on the subject, you could be denied a franking credit if you buy and sell shares within a 45-day period and you receive a franked dividend from the company. The good news is under the 'small shareholder exemption provisions' this nasty rule will not apply if the total franking credits you receive from your entire share portfolio is $5000 or less. As this can be a rather complex issue you should seek professional advice if your total franking credits exceed $5000. For more details see ATO fact sheet *Income from dividends*. You can download a copy from its website.

> **Handy tip**
>
> Getting a franked dividend is similar to a salary or wage earner having tax withheld from their gross pay. The franking credit is equivalent to the tax that was deducted from your gross pay, while the cash dividend is equivalent to you receiving your net pay. When you lodge your individual tax return you're liable to pay tax on your gross income and the tax that was withheld is applied against the net tax payable (which is exactly what happens when you get a franked dividend).

A company's capacity to pay franked dividends — particularly if they're fully franked — could become an important issue if you're investing predominantly for income. This is especially the case if you're a low income earner or a retiree relying on the dividend payments to fund your retirement. This is because if you get a refund of your franking credits the return on your investment will increase. The daily newspapers normally publish details of companies that pay franked dividends.

> **Case study: receiving a franked dividend**
>
> At the end of the financial year Anita received $12 000 interest from a term deposit and a $10 000 fully franked dividend from Crabtree Ltd.

Case study *(cont'd)*: receiving a franked dividend

The franking credit was $4285 (see figure 9.1). When Anita lodges her individual tax return she'll need to include the $10 000 dividend plus the $4285 franking credit as part of her taxable income. She also incurred $200 expenditure in deriving her dividends.

Individual tax return

Income

Interest		$12 000
Dividends	Franked amount	$10 000
	Franking credit	$4 285
Total income or loss		$26 285
Less:		
Interest and dividend deductions		$200
Taxable income		**$26 085**

Calculation of tax payable / refund

Tax Payable on $26 085	$3012
Plus	
1.5% Medicare levy	$391
	$3403
Less:	
Low income tax offset *	$1500
Franking credits	$4285
	$5785
Refund of tax	**$2382**

* Anita is also entitled to a $1500 low income tax offset — per 2010–11 tax rates.

Handy tip

If you get a lot of dividends you may need to prepare an 'Instalment Activity Statement' and pay tax more frequently, usually on a quarterly basis. The Australian Taxation Office will tell you if you need to do this. So to meet your legal obligations make sure you keep your shareholder dividend statements. The tax you pay is credited against your end of financial year assessment.

Dividend reinvestment plan

When you become a shareholder the company will normally send you details about their dividend reinvestment plan. If you make an election to participate, you'll receive additional shares in lieu of the dividend payment. These shares are generally issued to you at a discount (for example, 5 per cent below the current market price) and no brokerage fees are payable. This could prove a lucrative way of building up a quality share portfolio. As you're effectively buying more shares with your dividend payments, you're still liable to pay tax on the shares you receive in lieu of the dividend payment.

Capital gains tax: the rules you had to have

Capital gains tax (CGT) was introduced on 19 September 1985 and only applies to shares you acquire after this date. So if you're still holding shares you bought before this date that are making you a truckload of money, you won't have to pay CGT if you sell them today. On 21 September 1999 the government changed the rules for calculating a capital gain. Under the new system if you buy and sell shares within 12 months and you make a capital gain the entire gain is taxed. This gain is called a 'non-discount capital gain' (see figure 9.2, overleaf). So if you make a $10000 capital gain and your tax rate is 31.5 per cent tax you can only keep $6850 (ouch!). But the good news is you're only taxed on half the gain if you hold the shares for more than 12 months.

The balance is tax free. This gain is called a 'discount capital gain' (see figure 9.2). So there's a big incentive to keep shares that are making you money for at least 12 months. The part of the gain that's taxable is added to any other assessable income you derive (such as salary and wages, business profits and investment income), and you're liable to pay tax at your marginal rates (which can vary between 0 per cent and 45 per cent). Incidentally, if you made a capital loss (or you have prior year capital losses), you can deduct the loss from the capital gain you made.

Figure 9.2: capital gains on shares

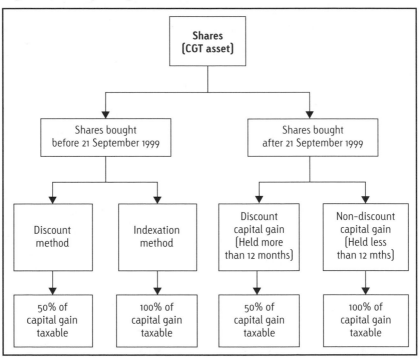

Handy tip

A capital loss on sale of one type of investment (for instance, shares) can be deducted from a capital gain you made on another type of investment (for instance, real estate).

Shares bought before 21 September 1999

If you own shares you bought before 21 September 1999 and you make a capital gain on sale, there are two ways to calculate a capital gain. They're called the 'discount method' and 'indexation method'. You can choose the method that will give you the best result. And that of course is the one that will result in you paying the least amount of tax!

⇒ *Discount method.* This method is identical to the way you calculate a capital gain today. In this case as you've held the shares for more than 12 months only half the gain is liable to tax. The balance is exempt (see figure 9.2).

⇒ *Indexation method.* Back in the good old days you were allowed to adjust your purchase costs (cost base) for inflation. This was done to eliminate having to pay tax on any gain that arose due to inflation. If you want to use this method you can only adjust for inflation from the date you bought the shares to 30 September 1999. As many years have now elapsed it's very unlikely that you'll use this method, as you'll generally find the discount method is the preferred option (see figure 9.2). I show you how this method works in chapter 13.

How to calculate a capital gain

In chapter 8 it was pointed out that when you buy shares you will get a buy contract note that will set out the date you bought the shares and your purchase costs (see chapter 8, figure 8.1). And when you sell your shares you will get a sell contract note that will set out the date you sold them, the costs you incurred to sell them, and the net proceeds on sale (see chapter 8, figure 8.3). So you'll need these two documents to check out how long you owned the shares and whether you had made a discount capital gain, a non-discount capital gain or a capital loss.

Case study: calculating a capital gain

Two years ago Alexei bought 1000 Crabtree Ltd shares at $6 per share and paid $100 purchase costs. According to the buy contract note he received from his stockbroker the total outlay was $6100. Today Alexei contacted his stockbroker and sold his 1000 Crabtree Ltd shares at $9 per share and paid $150 sale costs. According to the sell contract note the net proceeds on sale was $8850.

Capital proceeds (sale price)	$9000
Less:	
Cost base	
Purchase price	$6000
Purchase costs	$100
Sale costs	$150
	$6250
Net capital gain	**$2750**

Because Alexei held the shares for more than 12 months he's only liable to pay tax on half the gain, namely $1375. The other half is tax free. But if Alexei had bought and sold the shares within 12 months the entire gain ($2750) would have been liable to tax.

How to calculate a capital loss

If you make a capital loss on sale of a parcel of shares, unfortunately the capital loss can only be deducted from a capital gain. If you make no capital gains in the same financial year you incur the capital loss, you can offset the capital loss against any capital gains you may make in the future. So you'll need to keep a record of your capital losses. The following case study shows you how to calculate a capital loss.

Case study: calculating a capital loss

Two years ago Annette bought 1000 Apex Ltd shares at $7 per share and paid $100 purchase costs. According to the buy contract note she received from her stockbroker the total outlay was $7100. Today Annette contacted her stockbroker and sold her 1000 Apex Ltd shares at $2 per share and paid $50 sale costs. According to the sell contract note the net proceeds on sale was $1950.

Capital proceeds (sale price)	$2000
Less:	
Reduced cost base	
Purchase price	$7000
Purchase costs	$100
Sale costs	$50
	$7150
Capital loss	**$5150**

If you incur a capital loss and you also made a non-discount capital gain and a discount capital gain in the same financial year, make sure you deduct the capital loss (or any prior year losses) from your non-discount gains first. Otherwise, you could find yourself paying more tax than is necessary. This is because you can only claim a 50 per cent discount *after* any current and prior capital losses have been taken into account. So make sure you deduct your capital losses from your non-discount gains first as they do not qualify for the discount. If the loss was deducted from the discount capital gain first, you'll effectively lose the full value of the loss. By the way, if you find yourself in this situation there are no official rules regarding the order of claiming a capital loss. This is because the ATO leaves it up to you to make this decision. So it's important that you get this right at the outset. If you've not sure what to do you should seek professional advice.

The following case study shows you the correct way of calculating a net capital gain if you make discount and non-discount capital gains and a capital loss in the same financial year.

Case study: claiming a capital loss against capital gains

During the financial year Lee sold the following shares:

⇒ A parcel of Woolworths Ltd shares he had owned for more than 12 months. The capital gain on sale was $18 000.

⇒ A parcel of Westpac Ltd shares he had owned for less than 12 months. The capital gain on sale was $16 000.

⇒ A parcel of Telstra Ltd shares. The capital loss on sale was $18 000.

In this case Lee will need to separate the non-discount capital gain ($16 000) and discount capital gain ($18 000). With respect to the $18 000 capital loss he incurred, the loss should first be applied against the $16 000 non-discount capital gain as this gain does not qualify for the 50 per cent discount. Any loss that's left over (in this case $2000) is deducted from the $18 000 discount capital gain. As Lee is left with a net $16 000 discount capital gain, only 50 per cent of this amount ($8 000) is liable to tax.

	Non-discount capital gain	Discount capital gain
Woolworths Ltd		$18 000
Westpac Ltd	$16 000	
Less capital loss ($18 000)	$16 000	$2 000
	Nil	$16 000
Less 50% discount		$8 000
Net capital gain	$Nil	$8 000

On the other hand, if Lee had deducted the $18 000 capital loss from the $18 000 discount capital gain first, he would have been left with a $16 000 non-discount capital gain. Under these circumstances the entire amount is liable to tax, rather than $8000 if the $18 000 loss was first applied against the non-discount capital gain.

Taxing your brain: capital losses and franked dividends

In the following scenario did Ken incur a loss, break even or come out in front? (His marginal rate of tax is 30 per cent).

⇒ On 1 March Ken purchased 1000 shares at $34 per share ($34 000).

⇒ On 18 March the company declared a $1.40 fully franked dividend ($1400). The franking credit was $0.60 ($600).

⇒ On 20 April Ken decided to sell the shares at $32 per share ($32 000) and incurred a $2000 capital loss. The potential tax saving is $600 ($2000 × 30%).

Although Ken incurred a nasty $2000 capital loss on sale, when you take taxation into account, Ken had indirectly come out ahead as illustrated here:

Dividend payment	$1400
Franking credit	$600
Capital loss	($2000)
Potential tax saving on capital loss	$600
Net outcome	$600

Selling different parcels in same company

It can get a little tricky if you buy different parcels of shares in the same company on different occasions. This is because if you want to sell some shares down the track you'll need to know which parcel you sold in order to work out whether you had made a capital gain or capital loss. The following case study illustrates the dilemma you could face. If you make the wrong decision here you could find yourself paying tax unnecessarily.

Case study: selling different parcels

Over a period of three years Jason purchased 3000 Western Ltd shares. He has three buy contract notes on his table showing the following details:

⇒ 1000 Western Ltd shares   Total outlay $2000
   (purchased three years ago)

⇒ 1000 Western Ltd shares   Total outlay $6000
   (purchased two years ago)

⇒ 1000 Western Ltd shares   Total outlay $10 000
   (purchased one year ago)

Today Jason rang his stockbroker and sold 1000 Western Ltd shares. The sale price was $6000. The problem now is which shares did Jason sell?

⇒ If he chooses the shares he bought three years ago he will make a $4000 capital gain.

⇒ If he chooses the shares he bought two years ago he will come out square.

⇒ If he chooses the shares he bought one year ago he will incur a $4000 capital loss.

The parcel Jason will ultimately select will be the one that will give him the best result. For example, if he had made a $4000 capital gain on a previous transaction, it may be worth selling the parcel he purchased one years ago and declare a $4000 capital loss! The loss will offset the gain and no tax is payable on the gain he made. Incidentally, as Jason has kept proper records he can choose to sell say 500 shares he bought three years ago and 500 shares he purchased one year ago. Jason will need to choose which parcel of shares he intends to sell at time of sale.

Under the CGT provisions each parcel is treated as a separate asset with a different cost base. So as long as you can identify the shares you bought with the shares you sold there will be no problem. When you get a buy or sell contract note you will find a 'contract note number' on each contract (see chapter 8 figures 8.1 and 8.3). This is the number you will use to make that identification. Because Jason kept his three buy contract notes he can do this by merely choosing the appropriate buy contract note to identify the shares he bought with the shares he sold. (For more details see Taxation Determination TD 33 *Capital Gains: How do you identify individual shares within a holding of identical shares*).

Claiming a tax deduction

Under Australian tax law for an expense to be tax deductible a relevant connection must exist between the expenditure you incur and the derivation of your assessable income—in this case, the dividends you receive. The following expenses are typical examples of expenditure commonly associated with owning shares:

$ interest on borrowings to buy shares that pay dividends

$ bookkeeping and postage to manage your share portfolio

$ investment journals that provide information to help you manage your share portfolio

$ travel expenses to consult a stockbroker

$ travel expenses to attend a company's annual general meeting

$ costs of subscriptions to sharemarket information services provided it's for the purpose of deriving dividends

$ internet and data access costs incurred for share-trading activities

$ depreciation of share-trading software

$ mobile phone calls for a share trader to access live market information.

The brokerage costs and GST you incur at the time you buy and sell your shares are not tax deductible (unless you run a share-trading business). These costs are taken into account when calculating whether you had made a capital gain or capital loss on sale. (See case studies 'calculating a capital gain' and 'calculating a capital loss').

Borrowing to buy shares

A major expense you're likely to incur in the course of putting together a share portfolio is interest on borrowings. For interest to be a tax deductible expense there must be a reasonable expectation that you're likely to receive a dividend. So before you borrow money to buy shares in a particular company make sure you check the company's dividend payment history. If you find the company had never declared a dividend it's unlikely that you can claim a tax deduction. For example, this could arise if you buy shares in mining companies that don't declare dividends. Nevertheless, under the CGT provisions, your interest payments can be included as part of the share's cost base, and can be taken into account if you make a capital gain. Unfortunately, you can't use the interest expenditure to create or increase a capital loss. The following case study illustrates how this works.

Case study: non-deductible interest

Six months ago Franca borrowed $20 000. The purpose of the loan was to buy a parcel of shares in a gold-mining company. She checked the company's dividend payment history and found the company had never declared a dividend. She paid $20 000 for the shares and sold them today for $30 000. During the period of time Franca owned the shares, she paid $1000 interest, which was not tax deductible. Under these circumstances the interest can be added to the share's cost base ($20000) and can only be taken into account if she makes a capital gain. The capital gain Franca made on disposal is calculated as follows:

Capital proceeds (sale price)	$30000
Less:	
Cost base	
Purchase price	$20000
Non-deductible interest	$1000
	$21000
Capital gain	**$9000**

On the other hand, if the sale price was $15000 Franca would not be able to claim the $1000 interest she incurred, as it cannot be taken into account to create or increase a capital loss.

Share-trading business

A share trader is a person who regularly buys and sells shares with the intention to make a profit. Under Australian tax law you don't need an Australian Business Number (ABN) to quote to your stockbroker. Whether you're carrying on a share-trading business is a question of fact. The Australian Taxation Office examines the following to check whether you're a genuine share trader or investor:

⇒ your intention to make a profit

⇒ whether you're carrying out your activities in a business-like manner

⇒ whether you keep proper records

⇒ the amount of capital you've invested

⇒ whether you trade on a regular basis

⇒ the number of trades you do each year.

Share-trading business *(cont'd)*

You need to establish this because share traders are taxed differently to the way investors are taxed. As a general rule, the more trades you do the greater the chance you'll be classified as a share trader (for instance, you do 10 trades a week/520 trades a year). The benefit of being classified as a share trader is your trading losses can be deducted from any other assessable income you derive. An investor, on the other hand, can only deduct a capital loss from a current or future capital gain. The bad news is a share trader cannot claim a 50 per cent discount on gains made on shares held for more than 12 months. But this won't be a problem because it's unlikely a share trader will hold their shares for more than 12 months.

Chapter 10

Building a quality share portfolio

You've plucked up enough courage to start a share portfolio. You tentatively go to the business section of your daily newspaper and find more than 1500 companies listed on the Australian Securities Exchange (ASX). Shock! Horror! But don't panic. Building a share portfolio is not rocket science once you get the hang of it. So let's start on a positive note. As long as you invest sensibly, spread your risk and stick with the proven performers you'll soon find yourself heading in the right direction. In this chapter I chat about how to start a share portfolio and what you'll need to consider when choosing a company.

The rules you need to follow

Establishing a share portfolio should primarily be based on fulfilling your overall objectives (such as building wealth and loving it!). Ideally, your 'dream team' share portfolio should consist of a number of quality blue chips that can deliver capital growth and pay lots of dividends along the way (preferably fully franked). Which is easier said than done! In chapter 2 it was pointed out when you invest in the sharemarket you'll be relying on publicly listed companies running profitable businesses. And of course the more profit they make, the wealthier you're likely to become. There's an investment adage that you should 'build on what you know; don't buy what you don't understand'. So before you part with your hard-earned cash it's prudent that you understand what companies do to generate their profits, and check whether they're performing satisfactorily. A stockbroker can help you with this exercise. You can also get a reasonable idea of what they do if you read the company's annual report.

When putting together a share portfolio you should consider buying companies that operate in different sectors of the Australian economy (for instance, banking, insurance, retail, telecommunications and mining). There are many reasons for doing this:

$ We've all heard the saying you should never put all your eggs in one basket. To avoid any potential disasters that could literally wipe you out overnight, it's wise to buy shares in a number of companies. A manageable portfolio of around 10 companies might be worth exploring. A stockbroker or financial planner can help you choose an ideal number to suit your particular circumstances.

$ Having your fingers in many pies will allow you to take advantage of any favourable economic news — both domestic and overseas (especially from the US) — that could have a positive impact on company profits. For example, good economic news like an increase in demand for Australian resources could see the mining sector go through the roof, while a decrease in the Australian dollar could boost tourism in Australia.

$ The more companies you own the greater the chance of getting into something good. Put simply, you've got to be in it to win it—and, like buying raffle tickets, the more you hold the greater the chance that you could strike gold.

Before you jump into the deep end, a word of caution: it's reasonable to say not every company you select will turn out to be a winner. If you do happen to pull it off—besides laughing all the way to the bank—someone will probably erect a statue in your honour! Remember there's a strong possibility you could lose money if share prices fall. So if you find you're holding dead wood, instead of having a migraine worrying about it, you could consider doing a little pruning. In chapter 8 it was emphasised it only takes a few seconds to sell your shares—and, as if you had a magic wand—no more headache! It's as easy as that! By the way, taking a loss is not all doom and gloom. Before you think I must be going gaga saying this, under Australian tax law a capital loss can be deducted from a capital gain. When you do this you'll reduce paying tax on any capital gains you've made! In the meantime, the net proceeds on sale can be reinvested in another company that hopefully will increase in value. If you haven't made any capital gains the loss can be deducted from any capital gains you may make in the future (for more details see chapter 9).

Narrowing down your choices

It goes without saying the secret to building a quality share portfolio is finding companies that are going to make money for you. So how do you know which companies to buy? A good starting point is to check those companies that make up the Standard and Poor's ASX 200—referred to as the S&P/ASX 200 index. This index represents more than 90 per cent of the total market capitalisation of the Australian stock market. It is also the benchmark for measuring the investment performance of all the major managed funds in Australia. Market capitalisation is calculated by multiplying the company's current market price by the number of shares the company has issued. For example, if the current market price is $2 and the company has issued 12 billion shares, the company's market capitalisation is $24 billion. The various companies included in the index are published in the daily newspapers.

To narrow down your selections even further there is another handy index called the S&P/ASX 20 index. The companies that make up this index should all be well known to you (see table 10.1). The great bit about this index is it effectively represents more than half the entire wealth of the Australian economy. So if these companies fall by the wayside we'll all be in a pickle!

Table 10.1: S&P/ASX 20 index

Abbreviation	Company	Sector
(AMP)	AMP Ltd	Insurance
(ANZ)	ANZ Banking Group Ltd	Banks
(BHP)	BHP Billiton Ltd	Materials
(BXB)	Brambles Ltd	Commercial services & supplies
(CBA)	Commonwealth bank of Australia Ltd	Banks
(CSL)	CSL Ltd	Pharmaceuticals & biotechnology
(FGL)	Fosters Group Ltd	Food, beverage & tobacco
(MQG)	Macquarie Group Ltd	Banks
(NAB)	National Australia Bank Ltd	Banks

Abbreviation	Company	Sector
(NCM)	Newcrest Mining Ltd	Materials
(ORG)	Origin Energy Ltd	Energy
(QBE)	QBE Insurance Group Ltd	Insurance
(RIO)	Rio Tinto Ltd	Materials
(SUN)	Suncorp-Metway Ltd	Banks
(TLS)	Telstra Corporation Ltd	Telecommunications services
(WBC)	Westpac Banking Corporation	Banks
(WDC)	Westfield Group	Real Estate
(WES)	Wesfarmers Ltd	Food & staples retailing
(WOW)	Woolworths Ltd	Food & staples retailing
(WPL)	Woodside Petroleum Ltd	Energy

Source: CommSec.

For a small investor with a limited budget investing in companies that make up the S&P/ASX 20 index is not a bad way to kick-start a share portfolio. A stockbroker can help you select specific companies that are right for you. As mentioned in the previous section, it'll give you enough options to invest in quality blue chips from different sectors of the Australian economy. You'll also be investing in companies that you deal with every day (such as banking, insurance, retail and telecommunications companies). This can be very reassuring—especially if you happen to be one of their customers—as you'll know how they derive their profits. As you become more affluent you could consider expanding your share portfolio, or perhaps increasing the number of shares you currently own. By the way, the major domestic and world key market indices you're likely come across are set out in table 10.2 (overleaf).

Table 10.2: key market indices

Australia	United States	Asia	Europe
All Ordinaries Index	Dow Jones index	Nikkei (Tokyo)	FTSE (London)
S&P/ASX 200	Nasdaq	Hang Seng (Hong Kong)	DAX (Germany)
	S&P 500	Straits Times (Singapore)	CAC (Paris)

Investment adages

The following famous investment adages or sayings are often quoted by the experts to explain some general principles associated with investing in the stock market. These are not bad investment adages to keep in mind:

⇒ *Buy the dips, sell the rips:* meaning buy when the market goes down and sell when the market goes up.

⇒ *Buy the rumour, sell on the news:* meaning buy when you hear a rumour or believe that something could happen (for instance, strong profit growth), and sell when the news or facts are released.

⇒ *Sell in May and go away; come back in November:* meaning stock markets tend to slow down around May and become stronger again in November through to April.

⇒ *You'll never go broke taking a profit:* meaning you won't do any harm taking some profit off the table if you get the chance to do so.

⇒ *Scared money never wins:* meaning if you're scared of losing money or don't know what you're doing, don't invest.

⇒ *Time in the market is better than timing the market:* meaning it's extremely difficult to pick the bottom and top of the market; it's better to remain in the market over a given period of time.

⇒ *Past performance does not guarantee future results:* meaning what happened in the past does not necessarily imply that this will also be the case in the future.

⇒ *If you're going to panic, panic early:* meaning if you're planning on doing something (for instance, buy or sell), do it early.

⇒ *Sell into any rally:* meaning the best time to sell is when the market is rising. You may miss the boat if share prices suddenly fall.

⇒ *Don't try to catch a falling knife:* meaning avoid buying shares that are falling sharply in the hope that they will quickly rebound.

⇒ *Never marry a stock:* meaning your decision to buy or sell shares should be done on a strictly commercial basis.

⇒ *When even shoeshine boys are giving you stock tips you know it's time to sell:* meaning when everybody starts getting into the sharemarket it's a sign the market is overheating and it's time to get out.

Analysing a company

I always like using the analogy that analysing the performance of a company is similar to trying to back a winner in the Melbourne Cup. With tips coming from every direction, a shrewd punter would carefully study the form guide and listen to what the experts are saying. So before you buy shares in a particular company you should also study the 'form guide' and listen to what the experts—the stockbrokers—are saying about the companies you're keen to buy. The necessary details can be found in the company's annual report. Also, the business section in the daily newspapers and watching the business news on television (particularly the dedicated business channels on Foxtel) can give you a wealth of information. The following sections set out the 'big picture' issues you should consider.

Core business

Before you commit yourself to buying shares, it pays to do your own research and check what the company does to generate its sales and profits. Buying shares in companies when you do not understand what they do is full of danger. It's like driving blindfolded. A good starting point is to look for companies with established brand names who are the leaders in their industry. If these companies are not going too well you would think those down the pecking order would also be feeling the pinch! A stockbroker can help you identify companies' core business activities and explain what they do to generate sales. Some of the key issues you should take into account are:

$ *How long has it been in business?* This will tell you the company's ability to survive and trade under varying economic conditions.

$ *Who does it rely on for sales?* Is it from one major client or many clients? If it's from one major source, what would happen if it were to lose that client?

$ *Is it capable of changing direction to tap into new markets, trends and fads?* It's no use trying to sell products and services that no-one needs any more. For example, at the beginning of the 20th century building horse buggies was a thriving business until they invented the horseless carriage (car).

Competition

It's important that you identify who the company's main competitors are, as they could have an adverse impact on company profits. For example, if you're keen to invest in a particular bank, there are umpteen banks all trying to outdo one another. So you should check out whether the company's 'market share' (overall sales) is increasing or decreasing and what percentage of the total market it controls.

Management team

You should find out who's in charge and what experience they possess. This information is normally set in the company's annual report. Remember key decision makers can make or break a company, as they determine policy and set the agenda of the future direction of the company. A good management team is one that can continually find new ways of growing the business and make more profits.

Company profits

A key test of a good company is its ability to make lots of profits in a competitive market. Put simply, a company is valued by assessing its ability to maintain and increase its earnings and more particularly 'earnings per share'. You'll generally find share price movement (up or down) is dependent on profit forecasts. So you should check this out. For example, good news of positive earnings growth could push share prices through the roof, while a 'profit warning' of an impending decline in profits (or increased loss) could see share prices plunge. Earnings growth is primarily dependent on:

$ the continual demand for the company's goods and services (consumer spending)

$ whether current economic conditions are affecting the company's ability to trade profitably

$ its ability to grow the business (find new markets, domestic and overseas)

$ its capacity to increase prices and still remain competitive

$ its ability to reduce costs (operate more efficiently)

$ the level of growth in quality asset holdings (the source of future earnings growth).

Dividend policy

You should check out whether the company is paying dividends to shareholders (see chapter 11). This becomes an important issue if you're relying on the dividend payments to fund your lifestyle or you wish to borrow money to invest. Remember you can only claim a tax deduction if the shares you buy pay dividends. The sort of information you need to examine includes:

$ what percentage of the company's profits is distributed to shareholders

$ whether the dividend payments are increasing each financial year

$ the amount paid to shareholders—referred to as dividends per share

$ whether the dividends are fully franked.

Major shareholders

Companies normally publish a list of all the major shareholders in the company's annual report. They are the major stakeholders who will be keen to see the company does well. This list will tell you what percentage of the company they own and control, and whether they are capable of influencing company policy. If you see some 'big names' on the list, it can give you some sense of reassurance (as they stand to lose a packet if the company turns out to be a dud!).

Stockbroker recommendations

You should check out what the stockbrokers think about the company and read their newsletters. Stockbrokers will tell you whether the company is a 'buy', 'accumulate,' 'sell' or 'hold' stock. This is a good guide as to whether the company's share price is likely to rise or fall in the foreseeable future. It's also worth checking whether the company has a good credit rating (see table 10.3). For example, a AAA credit rating would indicate the company is very strong and trading satisfactorily, while a CCC credit rating would suggest the company is vulnerable. The major Australian companies listed on the ASX normally publish their respective credit ratings in their annual report.

Table 10.3: key Standard & Poor's credit ratings

AAA	Very strong
AA	Strong
A	Moderately strong
BBB	Adequate
CCC	Vulnerable
D	Defaulted

Companies and the economy

Financial analysts often describe a company as either a cyclical, growth or defensive stock to explain how they're likely to perform under different economic conditions.

Companies and the economy *(cont'd)*

⇒   *Cyclical stocks.* These are companies that rely on favourable economic cycles for earnings and capital growth. The earnings and growth prospects of cyclical companies tend to rise and fall in line with economic activity that could have a positive or negative impact on demand for their goods and services (for instance, the mining and banking sectors). Share valuations will tend to be relatively volatile.

⇒   *Growth stocks.* These are companies that operate in certain sectors of the economy that are constantly growing, which could have a positive impact on earnings and growth prospects (for instance, the technology sector). Companies will tend to retain much of their profits to help grow the business. Their price/earnings ratio is relatively high as investors anticipate good results (see chapter 11). Share valuations are likely to increase (but can quickly fall if it turns out to be a dud).

⇒   *Defensive stocks.* These are companies whose business activities are not adversely affected by changes in economic activity (for instance, the retail and health sectors). Their earnings and growth prospects tend to remain relatively stable whether the economy is booming or in decline. Share valuations will tend to be relatively stable.

Chapter 11

Doing your sums: understanding share ratios

Investing in shares to create wealth is primarily dependent on your ability to buy shares at bargain-basement prices that will hopefully make you lots of money. And of course the less you pay the more money you stand to make! Unfortunately, investing in the sharemarket is not an exact science and there's a risk you could pay more than what a share is theoretically worth. The good news is there are financial ratios that you can use to steer you in the right direction—so grab your calculator and read on! The financial ratios listed here are commonly used by financial planners and stockbrokers to examine whether a company is financially sound and profitable. They're also used to check whether you're likely to get value for your money. In this chapter I chat about the major financial ratios professionals employ to assess the financial viability of a company. These ratios are normally published in the daily newspapers and can also be found in the company's annual report.

Company's dividend policy

A company's capacity to pay dividends—particularly if they're fully franked—is an important issue to consider if you're investing predominantly for income. This is especially so if you happen to be a retiree looking for a steady and reliable income flow. The following ratios can help you track down specific companies that can meet this key objective.

Dividend yield

Formula: dividend per share ÷ market price × 100

Example: $0.35 ÷ $6.52 × 100 = 5.36 per cent

The dividend yield represents the return on your investment expressed as a percentage. Using the above example it is calculated by dividing the current market price ($6.52) into the dividend per share ($0.35) expressed as a percentage (5.36 per cent). A dividend yield of around 5 per cent is generally considered to be an acceptable rate of return on your investment in shares. When you check the dividend yields published in the daily newspapers you'll find they will fluctuate on a daily basis. This is because if the market price of a particular share were to rise you will have to pay more to get that dividend. Under these circumstances the dividend yield will fall. But the good news here is if the market price falls, the dividend yield will rise as you will be paying a lesser amount to get that dividend. Keep in mind once you buy your shares (for instance, you pay $6.52), the dividend yield is calculated on the amount you paid (for instance, 5.36 per cent).

The dividend yield published in newspapers is calculated on dividend payments that a company had previously declared.

This is fine if future dividend payments are to remain the same. To find out whether the dividend payment is likely to increase or decrease you'll need to check the 'projected dividend payment'. You can get this information from a stockbroker. For example, if the dividend payment is expected to increase (for instance, from 35 cents to 40 cents), the projected dividend yield will rise (for instance from, 5.36 per cent to 6.13 per cent). If this is found to be correct the return on your initial investment will increase. Conversely, if the dividend payment is expected to fall, you'll get a lesser return on your initial investment.

Grossed-up dividend yield

Formula: (dividend payment + franking credit) ÷ market price × 100

Example: ($0.35 + $0.15) ÷ $6.52 × 100 = 7.66 per cent

The grossed-up dividend yield is the company's pre-tax dividend yield. Using the above example it is calculated by dividing the current market price ($6.52) into the dividend per share ($0.35) plus the franking credit ($0.15) expressed as a percentage (7.66 per cent). In chapter 9 it was pointed out when a company declares a dividend it must tell you whether the dividend is fully franked, partially franked or unfranked. The term 'franked dividend' means the company has paid tax on its profits and as a consequence you will receive a franking credit. When you add these two amounts together the return on your investment will increase. Using the above example, if a company pays you a 35 cents cash dividend that's fully franked you will also get a 15 cents franking credit (see note 1, overleaf). As you are effectively getting 50 cents, the return of your investment will increase from 5.36 per cent (if the dividend wasn't franked) to 7.66 per cent. The grossed-up dividend yield (or pre-tax yield) is used to compare it against the pre-tax rate of return of other investments such as term deposits and rental properties (see chapter 5, case study: interest versus dividends).

Note 1: the formula to work out the franking credit is: cash dividend × 30 ÷ 70. So if you receive a 35 cents dividend fully franked, the franking credit is 15 cents ($0.35 × 30 ÷ 70). But if the dividend is partially franked (for instance, to 50 per cent), your franking credit is reduced to the extent that it's franked (for instance, from $0.15 to $0.075: $0.35 × 30 ÷ 70 × .50 = $0.075). Incidentally, 30 ÷ 70 is 'the company tax rate (0.30) ÷ (1 − the company tax rate: 0.70)'.

Handy tip

Under Australian tax law you'll need to include both the cash dividend and franking credit as part of your assessable income. You're liable to pay tax on the 'grossed-up' amount. The good news here is the franking credit can be used to reduce the net tax payable. If your franking credits exceed the net tax payable the Australian Taxation Office will refund the balance back to you!

Dividend cover

Formula: earnings per share ÷ dividend per share

Example: $0.70 ÷ $0.35 = 2

The dividend cover shows the number of times the company's current earnings can cover its dividend payments. Using the above example, it's calculated by dividing the dividend per share ($0.35) into the company's earnings per share ($0.70) and is used to check the company's dividend payment policy. In this case the result is two. By the way, if you reverse the formula you'll get the dividend payout ratio (see following). A dividend cover of two means the company is paying 50 per cent of its earnings to shareholders, so it has the capacity to increase the dividend payment. This becomes an important statistic if you're investing predominantly for income. It will also tell you whether a company can maintain and increase future dividend payments. So if you see the dividend cover is less than two, you'll know the payout ratio is more than 50 per cent, and if the dividend cover is more than two, the payout ratio is less than 50 per cent.

Handy tip

Newspapers use the following symbols in respect to dividend payments: [f] means the dividend is fully franked, [p] means the dividend is partially franked and no symbol implies the dividend is unfranked.

Dividend payout

Formula: dividend per share ÷ earnings per share × 100

Example: $0.35 ÷ $0.70 × 100 = 50 per cent

The dividend payout is the dividend cover expressed as a percentage and is used to check the company's current dividend payment policy. It's calculated by dividing the earnings per share ($0.70) into the company's dividend per share ($0.35) expressed as a percentage (50 per cent). This is important to know if you're investing predominantly for income. This is because it will tell you what percentage of the company's profits (earnings per share) is distributed to shareholders. It goes without saying the higher the dividend payout the better the return for investors. A dividend payout of around 75 per cent of the company's earnings would be considered an acceptable return to investors. The balance retained is normally used to help grow the business.

Company's financial stability

The following financial ratios are used to check whether a company is financially sound and profitable. In chapter 10 it was pointed out that share price growth is primarily dependent on a company's ability to grow its business and increase its earnings (profits). This becomes an important issue if you're investing predominantly for capital growth as earnings growth determines whether share valuations are likely to rise or fall.

Earnings per share (EPS)

Formula: net earnings ÷ ordinary shares issued

Example: $40 million ÷ 100 million = $0.40

Earnings per share are the net earnings (net profit) a company derives expressed on a per-share basis. It's calculated by dividing the total number of ordinary shares issued into the company's net earnings. Using the above example, if the company's net earnings are $40 million and it has issued 100 million ordinary shares, the EPS is 40 cents. So when you see this quoted in newspaper reports you'll know the company's generating 40 cents net profit for every ordinary share it has issued.

By the way, the EPS figure quoted in newspapers will remain the same until the company releases its next profit and loss report. A company's EPS can be used to measure the performance of a company over a given period of time. It can tell you:

$ whether the company's earnings per share is growing or falling

$ the dividend payout ratio (how much of the earnings is distributed to shareholders)

$ how the company is performing relative to other companies carrying on similar businesses.

Price/earnings ratio (P/E ratio)

Formula: market price ÷ earnings per share

Example: $6.52 ÷ $0.70 = 9.31

The price/earnings ratio shows the relationship of a company's current market price relative to its earnings per share (EPS). It is calculated by dividing the company's EPS ($0.70) into the company's market share price ($6.52). In the above example the P/E ratio is 9.31. This is used to check what the general market is willing to pay for every dollar the company earns (in this case 9.31 times profits). It's also used to check how long it will take for the company's earnings to cover its current market price (for instance, 9.31 years). As a rule of thumb the lower the P/E ratio the more attractive a company becomes. This ratio can be used to compare other companies carrying on similar businesses as well as the overall market. For example, if you find a company has a high P/E ratio (for instance, 50), it could suggest the shares are overpriced. This is especially the case if you find the P/E ratios of other companies carrying on similar businesses are trading at around 15. Under these circumstances the company will need to increase its earnings to justify its current market price. Otherwise there's a risk the share price could fall.

Return on shareholder's equity (ROE)

Formula: operating profit after tax ÷ shareholder's equity × 100

(Shareholder's equity (or book value) = assets − liabilities)

Example: $20 million ÷ $100 million × 100 = 20 per cent

The return on shareholder's equity (ROE) shows how effectively the company is managing shareholder's equity (or net assets) expressed as a percentage. It is calculated by dividing shareholder's equity into the company's operating profit after tax. Using the above example, if the company's operating profit after tax is $20 million and the company's shareholder's equity is $100 million, the ROE is 20 per cent. This ratio tells you the amount of profit a company can earn on the money shareholders had invested. In this case the company is earning 20 cents for every dollar that's invested in the company. A high ROE suggests the company is profitable while a low ROE suggests the company is less profitable. This ratio can be used to compare companies carrying on similar businesses.

Beta

Beta is determined by a complex mathematical formula and is used as a guide to help you assess the relative risk of a particular company. You can get this figure from a stockbroker. It's used to measure the volatility (risk) of the share price of a particular company relative to the general market.

⇒ If a company's Beta is 1, it indicates the company's share price is likely to fluctuate in line with the general market. So if the general market rises/falls by 10 per cent, the company's share price will most likely follow the trend.

⇒ If a company's Beta is less than 1, it indicates the company's share price is less volatile than the overall market. For example, if the company's Beta is quoted at 0.5, it implies if the general market rises/falls by 10 per cent, the company's share price will tend to rise or fall by 5 per cent.

⇒ If the company's Beta is more than 1, it indicates the company's share price is more volatile than the general market. For example, if the company's Beta is 2 it implies if the general market rises/falls by 10 per cent, the company's share price will tend to rise or fall by 20 per cent. This can be good news if the sharemarket is surging, as companies with a high Beta could deliver quick profits, but bad news if the sharemarket plunges.

Net tangible assets (NTA)

Formula: net tangible assets (NTA) = total assets – intangible assets (for instance, goodwill, patents and trademarks) – total liabilities

The NTA tells you the net worth (or book value) of a company expressed on a per-share basis, and is used to assess the value of a share. If the market price of a share is trading above its NTA you will be effectively paying more than what the company is theoretically worth. This could suggest the shares are overvalued. For example, if the market value is $18.50 and the company's NTA is $7.50, you'll be paying $11 more than what the company is theoretically worth. So if the company were to stop trading today and paid off all its debts you'll get back only $7.50. You'll generally find if the company is a quality blue chip, shareholders are prepared to pay the additional $11 premium, especially if the company is highly profitable and paying a good dividend yield. The NTA is also a good yardstick to check whether the company's share price is on a par with other companies carrying on similar businesses.

Price to net tangible assets (P/NTA)

Formula: market price ÷ net tangible assets

Example: $18.50 ÷ $7.50 = 2.46

This ratio shows the relationship of a company's market share price relative to its net tangible assets (NTA) and is used to assess the value of a share. It is calculated by dividing the company's NTA ($7.50) into the company's market share price ($18.50). In this example the company is trading at 2.46 times its NTA. The ratio can be used to check whether a company's share price is overvalued or undervalued. As a rule of thumb the higher the ratio the more expensive a company becomes. It's also used to check whether a company is on a par with other companies carrying on similar businesses. For example, if you find other similar companies are trading at around 1.75 times NTA it may suggest this company is overpriced. So if you accept 1.75 to be a more realistic price/NTA ratio the company's market price should be $13.12 ($7.50 × 1.75). On the other hand if you find the price/NTA ratio is less than 1 it could suggest:

$ the company may be a good buying opportunity

$ the company is trading below market expectations

$ the company's debts are rising in proportion to the company's assets.

Interest cover

Formula: operating profit ÷ interest paid

Example: $10 million ÷ $2 million = 5

Interest cover measures a company's ability to meet its interest commitments from current operating profits. It is calculated by dividing the company's interest payments ($2 million) into the company's operating profits ($10 million). In this case the company's operating profits are covering its interest payments five times. The interest cover tells you whether a company can increase its borrowing capacity and still service its loan repayments, especially the interest payments. The higher the interest coverage the less risk that the company is likely to become insolvent. Operating profits covering interest at least three times is considered to be a reasonable interest cover.

Debt-to-equity ratio

Formula: total liabilities ÷ shareholder's equity

Example: $40 million ÷ $140 million = 0.28

The debt-to-equity ratio is calculated by dividing the shareholder's equity ($140 million) into the company's total liabilities ($40 million). In this case it is 0.28 or 28 per cent. It is also used to check to what extent a company is relying on debt to finance its business operations (for instance, 28 per cent). A low debt-to-equity ratio suggests the company has the capacity to increase its exposure to debt to help grow its business. On the other hand, a high debt-to-equity ratio (for instance, over 50 per cent) would indicate the company is relying heavily on borrowed funds to finance its business operations. This is commonly referred to as highly geared (or leveraged). As a rule of thumb the higher the debt-to-equity ratio the greater the risk the company could get into financial difficulty down the track. This could quickly happen if company profits fall due to poor economic conditions and/or interest rate rise.

Fundamental analysis versus technical analysis

There are two competing methods to assess whether a company is undervalued or overvalued. They are known as 'fundamental analysis' and 'technical analysis'.

Fundamental analysis relies on historical data (such as a company's published financial reports) to check the financial stability of a company's business activities, and to determine whether its shares are likely to rise or fall. It uses economic data and financial ratios (for instance, price/earnings ratios and dividend yields) to determine a company's capacity to maintain and increase earnings and pay dividends in a highly competitive market.

Technical analysis, on the other hand, completely ignores a company's published financial reports. Rather, it uses share charts to assess share price trends and patterns to evaluate whether a company is undervalued or overvalued. It's also used to check whether a company's shares are likely to rise or fall, and when is the best time to buy and sell shares in the future. There are many different brands of software packages that technical analysts use to do this exercise.

Fundamental analysis versus technical analysis *(cont'd)*

Both methods can help you make a decision whether to buy or sell shares in a particular company. If you want to know more about technical analysis you can visit the website 'Incredible Charts' ‹www.incrediblecharts.com›.

Chapter 12

Staking out a claim: investing in property

When you invest in real estate you're effectively staking an exclusive claim to a piece of the Earth. While sitting in front of your PC, within a matter of seconds Google Earth can virtually zoom in from outer space and pinpoint the exact spot! A major limitation with investing in real estate is you need a substantial sum to buy it outright. As no two properties are identical a major dilemma is ensuring you don't pay more than what the property is worth. Doubts that you may have paid too much is a feeling you may experience. Welcome to the club! This is especially so if you're the highest bidder at an auction, and all your competitors have fallen by the wayside.

In this chapter I chat about the pros and cons of investing in real estate.

Checking out the good bits

The great bit about getting into bricks and mortar is it practically ticks all the right boxes of what constitutes a great investment. If you're wondering why this is so, here are the answers:

$ You'll derive rent if the property's leased. This is normally payable on a monthly basis.

$ Capital growth opportunities exist if property valuations rise. Property in a good location tends to double in value every seven to 10 years.

$ Under Australian tax law if you own a rental property or business premises, expenditure such as interest, rates, insurance, repairs and depreciation are tax deductible. You could also qualify for a capital works deduction (see chapter 13). Unfortunately, this won't be the case if you own non–income producing property such as your main residence or a holiday house that you use for your personal use and enjoyment.

$ You can put your property up as collateral to secure a loan that you can use to help grow your wealth.

Finding a suitable tenant

When you invest in real estate you'll be hoping to find a tenant to occupy your property and pay you lots of rent. This is particularly important if you're relying on the rental receipts to service your loan repayments or fund your current lifestyle. Finding a suitable tenant is primarily dependent on the terms of the lease, where the property's located and the lifestyle attractions that could appeal to potential tenants. A good real estate agent can help you find a suitable tenant: for comprehensive listings of real estate agents across Australia visit ‹www.domain.com.au› and click on 'Find an agent'.

Being aware of the risks

Although investing in real estate has some great features, to get a balanced view it's also prudent that you check out the risks and what could go wrong. As you'll be outlaying a substantial amount of capital, it's no use finding these things out after you've committed yourself.

$ *Expensive investment.* The first thing that'll hit you if you want to buy a property is the amount of capital you'll need to find. With median prices now at around the $500 000 mark, you may need to borrow a substantial sum. In the meantime, your lifestyle could be compromised while you're paying off the loan. Worse still, you'll be virtually putting all your eggs in one asset class basket.

$ *High entry and exist costs.* There are substantial costs associated with buying and selling property (for instance, stamp duty, GST and sale costs), which could run into thousands of dollars. In view of these costs you may need to hold your property for a number of years before you're likely to make a profit. And of course there is a risk that this may not happen.

$ *Stamp duty.* The amount you're liable to pay depends on the purchase price. If you want to know how much stamp duty you're up for in the state or territory where you reside, visit <www.domain.com.au> and go to 'News & Finance' then click on 'Finance calculators'.

$ *GST.* You could be liable to pay a 10 per cent goods and services tax (GST) if you buy a new residential property (or substantially renovated property) from a registered entity such as a property developer (see figure 12.1 on page 164). Incidentally, you can't claim a GST credit in respect of residential property used predominantly for residential accommodation as these transactions are classified as an 'input taxed supply'. This is not the case if you buy a commercial property and you're a registered GST entity. For more details read Australian Taxation Office publication *GST and Property*. You can get this from its website <www.ato.gov.au>.

$ *Sale costs.* When you sell a property you could be up for an agent's commission, advertising costs and legal fees. Incidentally, the real estate agent's commission to sell a property is normally around 2.5 per cent of the sale price.

$ *Liquidity.* As a property cannot be quickly sold, you may need to wait many months to get your hands on the cash, and the amount you'll get depends on what a potential buyer is prepared to pay you.

$ *Vacancy.* There's a risk your property could become vacant for a substantial period of time. This could be a major concern if you're relying on the rental payments to repay any loan you've taken out or to help maintain a reasonable standard of living.

$ *Ongoing costs.* There are ongoing costs associated with owning a property that you'll have to meet (for instance, land tax, rates, insurance and repairs), which could run into thousands of dollars each year.

$ *Low yielding investment.* As a general rule a rental property is a low-yielding investment as illustrated in the case study following. So it's important that your property increases in value to make this a worthwhile investment option.

Getting frustrated: ongoing costs

During one of my wealth creation courses a woman informed me she had 11 investment properties. Although this may sound great she was extremely depressed, as she was struggling to maintain a reasonable standard of living. This was because most of the rental income she was deriving was going towards paying off all the ongoing costs associated with owning these properties (particularly the massive land tax bill that states and territories impose on property investors). And when you take into account the tax she was liable to pay I could understand her concern. To reduce the burden it may be worthwhile diversifying into other asset classes such as shares and managed funds.

Case study: low-yielding investment

Chan paid $480 000 for an investment property and an additional $20 000 to cover stamp duty and legal fees. He currently receives $400 per week rent and his rental expenses are $3000 per annum (land tax, rates, insurance and repairs). Chan's marginal rate of tax plus Medicare levy is 31.5 per cent.

Purchase price	$480 000
Purchase costs	$20 000
Total outlay	**$500 000**
Gross rent	$20 800 per annum
Rental expenses	$3000 per annum
Return after expenses	$17 800 ($20 800 less $3000)
Tax payable (31.5%)	$5607
Net rent after tax	$12 193 ($17 800 less $5607)
Gross yield	4.16% ($20 800 ÷ $500 000 × 100)
Net yield	3.56% ($17 800 ÷ $500 000 × 100)
Net return after tax	**2.43%** ($12 193 ÷ $500 000 × 100)

Figure 12.1: real estate and GST

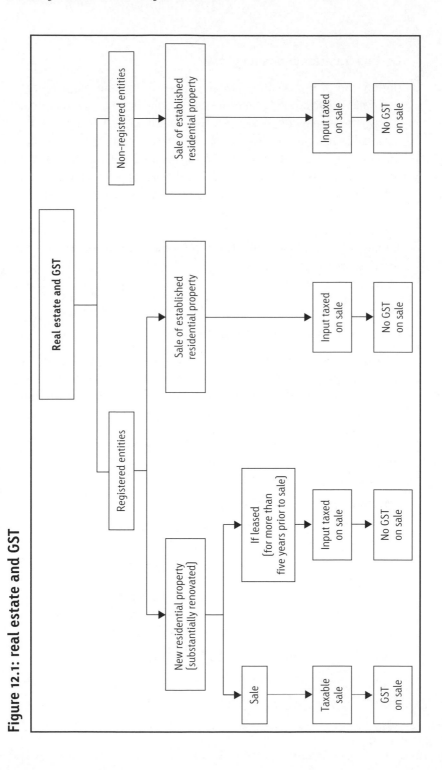

Examining three key issues

Generally, there are three key issues associated with investing in real estate. The tricky bit is trying to get all the components working smoothly, like a Swiss clock. These three issues are:

1 finding a suitable property

2 determining market price

3 raising the necessary finance.

Finding a suitable property

As every real estate agent or auctioneer worth their salt will testify, there're only three things you need to worry about: location, location and location. If you can get this important component right you'll generally find the rest of the bits of the jigsaw puzzle will quickly fall into place. So what are the key indicators to suggest you're buying in the right location? The answer will depend on whether you intend to buy a residential property (for instance, a house or apartment) or commercial property such as office space, a shop or a factory. Generally speaking, people tend to buy in suburbs they're familiar with; for example, because they've lived in these locations all their life and feel comfortable with the surroundings and/or have family and friends close by.

Residential property

If your preference is to invest in a residential property (house or apartment), you'll be hoping to entice a suitable tenant to reside there and pay you lots of rent. As this could be their home for some considerable time, it's important that the property is close to all conveniences such as public transport (buses, trams and trains), employment centres, hospitals and major shopping centres. If your tenant happens to be a family unit they'll also be keen to be close to public and private schools, child-minding centres, religious centres, sporting venues and parks and gardens. And if the property is close to a beach, lake or river you'll hit the jackpot. It's reasonable to say the better the location (and more attractions) the greater the chance your property will appreciate in value, as other potential buyers will be keen to buy it from you. As a rule of thumb property in good locations tends to double in value every seven to 10 years. By the way, under Australian tax law your main residence is exempt from tax. This could turn out to be a nice little earner if your home happens to be in a much-sought-after suburb where property valuations are continually rising.

When doing the rounds looking for a suitable residential property to buy, keep in mind the following:

$ Check out the size of the block of land the property's situated on — the bigger the better! This will give you the option to extend or subdivide down the track. You'll generally find land tends to appreciate in value over time while buildings tend to deteriorate and depreciate with age. So the bigger the block the bigger the pile of money you stand to make if you decide to sell.

$ Check out the building's structure with a fine tooth comb as it's no fun buying someone else's headaches. Potential repairs such as stumping, re-roofing, painting, rising damp, plumbing, guttering, cracks and pest control can cost a truckload of money to rectify. You can get a 'pre-purchase property inspection report' from a professional builder that will check these things out for you. Unfortunately, under Australian tax law initial repairs to a newly acquired property you intend to lease are not tax deductible. Nevertheless, they can be added to the purchase price and can be written off under the capital works provisions (see chapter 13).

$ Check out the general condition of the kitchen and bathroom. Speaking from personal experience, they tend to quickly age and are very expensive to modernise.

$ Check out the front and back yard, and more particularly the fences, the state of the garden and entertainment areas. Landscaping can cost heaps.

$ Check out the parking facilities. This becomes an important issue if you (or family members) own more than one car and car-parking spots are at a premium or difficult to find.

$ Check out the chattels. These are things like dishwashers, refrigerators, stoves, carpets, curtains and blinds that normally come with the property. Under Australian tax law these items are depreciable if you lease the property (see chapter 13).

$ There's an old saying that a good investment opportunity is to buy the worst house in the best street. So check out the neighbourhood and particularly the quality of the properties (and streetscape) in the location or suburb in which you intend to buy. This can add to the value and desirability of your property.

Checklist: useful publications and websites

⇒   *Rental properties* (NAT 1729), Australian Taxation Office ‹www.ato.gov.au›

⇒   *A guide for buyers and sellers,* Consumer Affairs Victoria ‹www.consumer.vic.gov.au›

⇒   *Price advertising for residential property sales,* Consumer Affairs Victoria ‹www.consumer.vic.gov.au›

⇒   *Buying property,* NSW Office of Fair Trading ‹www.fairtrading.nsw.gov.au›

> **Checklist *(cont'd)*: useful publications and websites**
>
> ⇒   *Costs associated with buying a property*, Real Estate Institute of Australia ‹www.reia.com.au›
>
> ⇒   ‹www.propertyguide.com.au/rural›, 'Domainrural', Australia's rural property guide

Commercial property

Investing in commercial property could prove a good way of deriving a steady and reliable income flow. Commercial property can include:

$ retail, such as shops, shopping centres and cinemas

$ office accommodation, suitable for professional bodies such as legal and accounting firms

$ industrial, such as factories for small business entities and warehouses

$ rural, and more particularly farms.

When you invest in commercial property the leases will tend to be long term (for instance, 10 years), and the annual return is generally around seven per cent before tax. The great bit here is your tenant is normally liable for ongoing costs such as rates, insurance and repairs. The amount of rent you can charge is usually calculated on an area basis with built-in annual reviews (for instance, in line with CPI increases). Incidentally, this is not the case with residential property. Further, you may need to register for GST as the transaction will be a taxable supply. If this is so you can claim a GST credit in respect to any GST you're charged on your own acquisitions. Success with this category of investment is primarily dependent on your tenant's capacity to run a profitable business from your premises. This could be great news when the economy is booming. There are three major limitations or risks you'll need to consider, namely:

$ *interest on loan.* The interest rates on a loan will tend to be higher than a residential property as there is a higher risk of default.

$ *long-term vacancy.* If your tenant leaves (for instance, due to a slowdown in economic activity), there's a risk your property could remain vacant for some considerable time. This could have an adverse impact on your cash flow.

$ *periodic refurbishment.* You may incur high refurbishment costs (such as regular maintenance of lifts) to meet ongoing occupational health and safety standards.

Handy tip

Under Australian tax law if you have a self managed super fund (SMSF), your super fund can own your 'business real property' (meaning your businesses premises) and lease it back to you at a commercial rate of rent. For more details see Tax Office guidelines *What constitutes business real property in respect to SMSF* (SMSFR 2009/1).

If you plan to invest in a commercial property the following may be worth examining. It goes without saying the more pluses you have up your sleeve the better the chances of finding a suitable tenant:

$ it's in a commercial centre

$ it's readily accessible to customers

$ it has adequate parking spaces for customers

$ it's near established infrastructure (such as roads, rail, shipping and airports)

$ the building can cope with modern technological requirements and will satisfy human comforts (for instance, meet occupational health and safety standards).

Handy tip

The construction cost of industrial buildings and structural improvements qualify for a four per cent capital works deduction. This means you can write off the cost of your construction costs at the rate of 4 per cent per annum. (Incidentally, the rate for a residential property is 2.5 per cent per annum.) To qualify the building must be used to derive assessable income. For more details read Tax Office publication *Rental properties* (NAT 1729).

Determining market price

A major dilemma with investing in real estate is no two properties are identical (unless you're buying an apartment). Trying to assess the correct market value of a particular property can be difficult. There are often major discrepancies between the advertised sale price and the actual sale price (particularly at an auction). It can be very frustrating if the discrepancy between the advertised price guide (for instance, between $400 000 and $450 000) and the actual sale price (for instance, $525 000) is miles apart. It can also be quite upsetting if you've spent money on getting a pre-purchase property inspection report.

There are many factors that can influence the market price of a property. The main ones are listed here:

$ *Location.* Location will play a key role in influencing market price, especially inner urban properties close to established infrastructure and properties near a beach or river.

$ *Quality of dwelling.* The more appealingly a property is portrayed to a potential buyer the more they may pay.

$ *Movement in interest rates.* This can influence a person's ability to borrow and service the loan repayments.

$ *Government incentives.* Incentives such as the first home owner's grants, home savings accounts and reduced stamp duty can encourage people to buy or build a property.

$ *Supply and demand.* The number of properties that are currently up for sale in a particular suburb or area will influence market price.

So what should you do to ensure you're getting value for money? Fortunately, there are a number of ways you can check the market value of properties that are currently on the market.

Median price

A good starting point is to check out the median price of properties that have been sold over a period of time. The median price is normally published in newspapers or you can find it on the internet. This will help you determine whether you can afford to buy in a particular location. By the way, the median price is the middle price of a number of reported sales in a particular suburb that had been put in order from highest to lowest. For example, there were 50 reported sales in the last three months in the particular suburb you're keen on. The highest reported sale was $925 000 and the lowest was $375 000. If the 25th property on the list of highest to lowest sale prices was $540 000 — then this is median price. The median price can be used to assess important issues such as market direction, whether prices are rising or falling and the rate of increase or decrease. One small exercise you could do is check out the most expensive properties to see what you stand to gain (for instance, big block, established garden, magnificent views). Next check out the most affordable to see why they're going so cheap (for instance, on a small block and building in a poor state of repair). You will now be in a better position to assess properties that are around the median price range.

Handy tip

Each quarter Australian Property Monitors publishes the median prices of houses and apartments in the major cities throughout Australia. For more details you can visit its website ‹www.homeprice guide.com.au›. You can also get this information from the Real Estate Institute of Australia website ‹www.reiaustralia.com.au›, especially the median prices of specific suburbs in the state or territory where you reside.

Check auction results

You should check the newspapers regarding the clearance rate of properties that were put up for auction. For example, 30 properties were put on the market last weekend and 21 were sold. You should also keep a note of their respective sale prices. You could also conduct a 'kerbside' inspection to see why they were sold at a certain price. This little exercise can be used to assess relative demand and recent sale price trends.

Consult the professionals

Visit the local real estate agents and check out the prices of properties that are up for sale. They can arrange a suitable time for you to inspect any property you may be keen to buy. They can also give you advice about price trends in locations in which you're interested in buying. It's also possible for you to find out 'actual sale prices' of properties in specific streets/ suburbs from fee-based services such as Australian Property Monitors <www.homepriceguide.com.au> and RP Data Australia <www.reports.rpdata.com.au>. By the way, a handy website you can visit is <www.domain.com.au>: it can give you a wealth of information about properties that are currently on the market throughout Australia.

Attend auctions

One great thing about attending an auction is you can inspect the property that's up for sale shortly before the auction commences. This will allow you to make a ballpark assessment of what you think the property's worth. The great bit here is if the property is sold, you will know within half an hour what the sale price was, and you can compare the result with what you consider it was worth. After you've attended a number of auctions you'll start to get a good idea about property valuations.

Checklist: useful websites

⇒ Property Reports from Domain.com: ‹www.domain.com.au›

⇒ Australian Property Monitors: ‹www.homepriceguide.com.au›

⇒ Property reports for the state of Victoria: ‹www.land.vic.gov.au› [search by address]

Raising the necessary finance

Getting into real estate can be an extremely difficult exercise, as you may need to borrow a substantial sum to cover the purchase price and all your costs (for instance, stamp duty, GST and legal fees). When financial institutions lend money they will check whether you're able to repay the loan. They will also get an independent property valuation. If they find the property is worth less than what you paid there is a risk you may not get the full amount.

Loan-to-valuation ratio (LVR)

This is a ratio between the size of your loan and the value of the security you're offering (for instance, the market value of your property). It's used by financial institutions to assess whether you're capable of servicing the loan expressed as a percentage. This is normally set at between 70 to 90 per cent of the value of your property. This ratio can also be used to help you work out how much you need to save for a deposit. For example, if the market value of your property is $450 000 and the LVR is 70 per cent, you'll need to save $135 000 for a deposit:

Market value of property	$450 000
Less:	
LVR set at 70%	$315 000
Required deposit	**$135 000**

Financial institutions have loan repayment calculators to help you work out your periodical payments (for instance, the financial calculators on website <www.domain.com.au>). This amount will depend on the following key variables, for example:

The loan amount	$315 000
Basis of repayments	Principal and interest
The term of the loan	20 years
Interest rate	7%
Periodical payments	Fortnightly

When you insert these variables into the loan repayment calculator your interest and principal repayments will amount to $1127 per fortnight.

Handy tip

If your deposit is less than 20 per cent of the value of your property you could be liable to pay a one-off 'lenders mortgage insurance' premium. This is to protect the financial institution in the event of you defaulting on your loan repayments. The amount you'll pay depends on how much you borrow. For example, if you borrow $350 000 the lenders mortgage insurance is about $4000.

Household income affordability test

Household income is the income a single or couple derives from all sources. As a rule of thumb your property repayments should not exceed 30 per cent of your household income. And the purchase price should not exceed four times your household income. For example, if your household income is $120000, your property repayments should not exceed $36000 per annum ($1385 per fortnight) and the purchase price should not exceed $480000. So it's prudent that you build into your repayment calculations a margin of safety to cover any possible contingencies such as an increase in interest rates and/or a potential fall in household income.

Saving for a deposit

If you are a first home buyer the federal government has two schemes to help you save for a deposit. They are as follows:

⇒ First home buyer grant, where the federal government will give you a one-off payment. At the time of writing the amount was $7000. For more details you can visit ‹www.firsthome.gov.au›.

⇒ First home saver accounts, where the federal government will make a contribution to a first home saver account if you also make a contribution. At the time of writing the maximum was $850 per annum if you made a $5000 contribution (being 17 per cent of the amount you contributed). For more details you can visit ‹www.firsthomesaver.com.au›.

Renovating properties

Under Australian tax law if you plan to buy a rundown property, fix it up and sell it at an enhanced price, you could be considered to be running a business of renovating properties. There are a number of tests the Tax Office uses to check whether this is the case. The main ones are:

$ the size and scale of your operations

$ whether you have the intention to make a profit (which is normally the case)

$ how often you buy and sell properties (the more you do the greater the chance you'll be considered to be running a business)

$ the amount of capital investment in the property venture

$ whether you're carrying on your activities in a business-like manner (for instance, keeping proper records, getting the required permits, raising the necessary finance)

$ whether you're carrying on your activities on a full-time or part-time basis

$ the degree of skill and knowledge you possess.

If you are carrying on a business you may need to register for GST. This will be the case if your annual turnover (sales) is more than $75 000 per annum. If you make a net profit on sale the entire net profit is liable to income tax. On the other hand, if you make a loss you can claim the loss as a tax deduction. But if the facts suggest you're not carrying on a business any capital gain or capital loss you make on sale will be taxed under the capital gains tax provisions (see chapter 13). For more details read the Australian Taxation Office publication *Are you in the business of renovating properties?* You can get a copy from your local Tax Office or you can download a copy from its website <www.ato. gov.au>.

Chapter 13

Taxing your property transactions

Under Australian tax law if you buy an income-producing property, the expenses you incur are normally tax deductible. Unfortunately, the trade-off is you're taxed on the rental income you receive, and you're up for capital gains tax (CGT) if you make a profit on sale. You're also up for CGT if you own a property (for instance, a holiday home) that you keep for your personal use and enjoyment. Although you can't claim expenses relating to your main residence (for instance, interest on a home loan), the good news is any profit you make on the sale is exempt from tax. This could prove a lucrative way of building wealth if your house appreciates in value (see chapter 14). In this chapter I chat about the major tax issues associated with owning a rental property.

Taxing your rent

Under Australian tax law, if you lease a property the rental income you receive from your tenant is normally liable to tax when it's paid to you. If the rent you collect is substantial you may need to prepare quarterly 'Instalment Activity Statements' disclosing the amount of rent you receive and tax you pay on an ongoing basis. The Tax Office will notify you if you have to do this. To meet your legal obligations you will have to keep accurate records of the rent you receive (for instance, the rental statements you receive from a real estate agent). The tax you pay is credited against your end of financial year assessment. If you lease a residential property used predominantly for residential accommodation, you don't need to get an Australian Business Number (ABN) to quote to your tenant. Also, under the GST provisions if you lease a residential property used predominantly for residential accommodation the transaction is classified as an 'input tax supply'. This means you can't charge GST on the rent you collect from your tenant, and you can't claim a GST credit on the GST you incur on your rental expenses.

Claiming rental deductions

As is the case with interest and dividend receipts, for an expense to be tax deductible a relevant connection must exist between the expenditure you incur and the derivation of your assessable income (in this case rent). If you lease a property make sure you charge your tenant a commercial rate of rent. Otherwise, the Tax Office could disallow your expenditure or reduce it to an amount that's considered reasonable. For example, you own a rental property where you could easily get $500 per week rent, but you decide to lease it to your son for $10 per week. If your annual rental expenses were $25 000, you'll most likely find that you won't be able to claim the full amount, as you're not charging your son a commercial rate. Further, you can only claim a tax deduction during the period your property is leased or is 'genuinely available for rent' (for example, a real estate agent is currently advertising for a prospective tenant). And if your property is only partly used to derive rent (for instance, you lease one room), you can only claim a part deduction. The following outlays are examples of the types of rental expenses associated with deriving rent:

$ administration costs

$ advertising to find a tenant

$ agent's commission to collect the rent

$ body corporate fees

$ borrowing expenses

$ capital works deduction

$ council rates

$ depreciation

$ gardening and lawn mowing

$ insurance on the building

$ interest on a loan

$ land taxes

$ legal expenses associated with preparing a lease

$ pest control

$ repairs and maintenance

$ travel costs (for example, to inspect your property, collect rent, undertake repairs)

$ water and sewage charges.

Handy tip

The ATO has issued free of charge the following comprehensive guidelines on the taxation of rental properties. You can download these guidelines from the ATO website ‹www.ato.gov.au›.

⇒ *Rental properties — claiming repairs and maintenance* (NAT 72841)

⇒ *Rental properties — claiming borrowing expenses* (NAT 71958)

⇒ *Rental properties — claiming legal expenses* (NAT 71956)

⇒ *Rental expenses — claiming capital works deductions* (NAT 72840)

⇒ *Rental properties — avoiding common mistakes* (NAT 71820)

⇒ *Rental properties* (NAT 1729)

⇒ *Guide to depreciating assets* (NAT 1996)

⇒ *Guide to capital gains tax* (NAT 4151)

Who said you can't get blood from a stone?

There are three specific types of expenses commonly linked with deriving rental income that you can claim. They are depreciation, capital works deductions and repairs. To qualify for these deductions there are certain tax rules you'll need to satisfy.

Depreciation

Depreciation is reducing the value of items you use to derive rental income due to wear and tear over the years. Incidentally, the Tax Office uses the term 'decline in value' rather than depreciation. Under Australian tax law you can depreciate items such as carpets, curtains and blinds, furniture, dishwashers, refrigerators, stoves and washing machines. The Tax Office publishes a comprehensive list of specific items that you can depreciate. When working out how much depreciation you can claim each year you can use a rate of depreciation based on the item's estimated effective life or you can use the Tax Office–recommended rates. I personally like using the Tax Office–published rates as the information is readily at hand. The bad news is there are certain items that you can't depreciate. For instance, you can't depreciate built-in kitchen cupboards, in-ground swimming pools, saunas and spas. This is because the Tax Office takes the view that these items form part of the building structure and are capital in nature and not tax deductible. Although you can't claim them as a depreciation expense, you can claim them under the 'capital works provisions' (more about this matter later). Incidentally, if you buy an item that costs $300 or less, you can claim the expenditure outright in the financial year you incur the outlay. This is on the proviso that you earn non-business income such as rent from a rental property.

There are two ways you can calculate a depreciation expense for tax purposes: they are the Prime Cost Method (PCM) and the Diminishing Value Method (DVM). If you use PCM you can claim a fixed amount each year until the depreciable item is written off. On the other hand, under DVM you will claim a bigger amount in the earlier years and a lesser amount in later years. The method you'll choose will depend on how quickly you want to write off your depreciable items. DVM is generally considered the better option as you can recoup your initial outlay at a faster rate. When choosing which method to use keep in mind the rate of depreciation under DVM is always twice the rate under PCM. For example, if the rate of depreciation is 15 per cent under the PCM method, the rate is automatically 30 per cent under DVM. For more details see Tax Office publication *Guide to depreciating assets* (NAT 1996). Incidentally, this publication has a good example of a worksheet that you can use to record all your depreciating assets. The following case study shows you how to calculate a depreciation deduction under both methods.

Case study: claiming a depreciation expense

On 1 July 2010 Lisa paid $5000 for a new high-tech electric oven for her rental apartment. She estimates its effective life is eight years. If she uses PCM the rate of depreciation is 12.5 per cent (100 per cent ÷ eight years = 12.5 per cent). But if she uses DVM the rate will double to 25 per cent (being twice PCM). The amounts Lisa can claim each year under either method are shown below:

	PCM (12.5%)	DVM (25%)
Electric oven (1 July 2010)	$5000	$5000
Decline in value (depreciation) (2011)	$625	$1250
Adjusted value	$4375	$3750
Decline in value (depreciation) (2012)	$625	$938
Adjusted value	$3750	$2812
Decline in value (depreciation) (2013)	$625	$703
Adjusted value	$3125	$2109

And so on until the electric oven is written off.

Keep in mind if you buy a depreciable asset part way through the year you must pro-rata the depreciation deduction in the first financial year you buy it. For example, if Lisa purchased the electric oven on 1 October 2010 she will only be entitled to claim nine months' depreciation in the 2010–11 financial year.

Handy tip

Under tax law there is a special method called 'low value pools' that you can use for items that cost less than $1000. This method allows you to use DVM and you can depreciate these items at the rate of 37.5 per cent. For more details see the ATO's *Guide to depreciating assets*.

Capital works deductions

Under Australia tax law if you buy an investment property the transaction is considered to be capital in nature and not a tax deductible expense. However, all is not lost because you can claim a special (statutory) tax deduction under the capital works provisions. Under these provisions you can claim a 2.5 per cent capital works deduction over a 40-year period. It applies to certain construction expenditure relating to income-producing buildings that commenced to be constructed after 15 September 1987. For example, you buy a new rental property that was constructed in 2010. If the eligible construction expenditure is $200 000 you can claim $5000 each year for the next 40 years. This may sound great. But the trade-off here is you have to deduct the amount you claim each year from the property's cost base (purchase price). This rule applies to rental properties you purchase after 13 May 1997 (see following for more details). If the construction commenced between 22 August 1984 and 15 September 1987 the annual rate is 4 per cent. This special (statutory) tax deduction also applies to any structural improvements or alterations you make to your property; for example, you decide to build an extra room or you make substantial renovations to your existing property. Incidentally, if you buy an established property that you intend to lease the annual deductions not yet claimed can be passed on to you. So you'll need to find out the building's construction costs at the time you buy the property. If this is unknown you can get an estimate from a qualified person (for instance, a quantity surveyor).

Construction expenditure

You can claim construction expenditure in respect to:

$ buildings

$ extensions (for instance, you add a extra room or build a garage)

$ alterations (for instance, you remove an internal wall)

$ structural improvements (for instance, you add a carport, sealed driveway, retaining wall or fence).

What you can't claim:

$ the cost of the land

$ expenditure on clearing land prior to construction

$ expenditure on landscaping.

Handy tip

If you buy a rental property after 13 May 1997, the amount of any capital works deductions you claim each year must be deducted from the property's cost base. Unfortunately, when you do this, you will increase the size of any potential capital gain you make on sale as illustrated in the following case study.

Case study: reducing the cost base

Five years ago Maria paid $500000 for a new rental property. At the time she bought the property she was advised the construction cost of the building for the purposes of claiming a 2.5 per cent capital works deduction was $200000. This means she can claim a $5000 per annum tax deduction for the next 40 years. Maria sold the property today and received $800000. During the period of time Maria leased the property the total amount of capital works deductions she claimed amounted to $25000 ($5000 × five years). Unfortunately, as Maria purchased the property after 13 May 1997 she will need to reduce the property's cost base by $25000. This will effectively increase the size of the capital gain that will be liable to tax (yuck!).

Sale price		$800 000
Less:		
Cost base		
Purchase price	$500 000	
Less:		
Capital works deductions	$25 000	$475 000
Net capital gain		**$325 000**

Although Maria has to pay more tax, as the property had been owned for more than 12 month only half the capital gain is taxed (see Capital gains tax, later in the chapter for more details).

Repairs

A major expense you're likely to incur if you own a rental property is ongoing repairs and maintenance. To help you understand what a repair is, the Tax Office has stated in its official publications that a 'repair for the most part is occasional and partial. It involves restoration of the efficiency of function of the property being repaired without changing its character and may include restoration to its former appearance, form, state or condition'. What all this means is if you're planning on repairing an item, make sure you merely restore it back to its previous condition, and don't make any improvements along the way; for example, you replace a couple of rusted galvanised roof sheeting with new ones. This is because if you improve an item rather than just repair it, the expenditure is considered capital in nature and not tax deductible: for example, you find your rusted galvanised roof is leaking like a sieve; rather than replace the damaged parts with new parts you decide to replace the entire tin roof with terracotta tiles that are more efficient and durable. Although you may have stopped the roof from leaking, under tax law you've effectively made an improvement and changed its character. Although you can't claim the expenditure as a repair you can claim it under the capital works deductions provisions.

By the way, if you buy a rental property and you find you need to do some repairs at the time you buy it (for instance, you decide to replace the rusted spouting or paint all the rooms), under tax law these repairs are classified as 'initial repairs' and are not tax deductible. This is because the need for these repairs did not arise during the time you owned the property. As these repairs arose during the time the previous owner owned the property, they are classified as capital in nature. But the good news here is these costs can be claimed under the capital works provisions.

> **Handy tip**
>
> The Australian Taxation Office has issued two important Taxation Rulings to explain the meaning of repairs. They are *Income tax: deductions for repairs* (TR 97/23) and *Income tax: capital gains: may initial repair expenditure incurred after the acquisition of a CGT asset be included in the relevant cost base of the asset?* (TD 98/19). You can get a copy from the Tax Office website ‹www.ato.gov.au›.

Goods and services tax

The goods and services tax (GST) is a broad-based tax of 10 per cent on most goods and services sold or consumed in Australia. With respect to real estate you're generally liable to pay GST if you buy new property (or one that has been substantially renovated) from a registered entity such as a property developer. If you lease a commercial property you may need to register for GST and collect GST from your tenant. If this is so, you can claim a GST credit in respect to any GST you were charged on your own acquisitions. This is also the case if you buy a commercial property. On the other hand, if you lease a residential property used predominantly for residential accommodation, the transaction is classified as an 'input tax supply'. This means you cannot charge your tenant GST on the rent you collect, and you cannot claim a GST credit in respect of any expenditure you incur. The ATO has published a booklet called *GST and property* (NAT 72957), which explains how GST applies to property sales and transactions. For more details you can visit the ATO website <www.ato.gov.au>.

Capital gains tax

The capital gains tax (CGT) provisions apply to CGT assets such as real estate that you buy on or after 20 September 1985. One notable exception is your main residence, which is exempt from tax. This means you won't be liable to pay CGT if you make a capital gain on sale (see chapter 14). With respect to property you bought before 20 September 1985, no CGT is payable if you make a capital gain on sale. This is because any assets you acquired before this date are excluded from the CGT provisions.

Property bought after 21 September 1999

The way you calculate a capital gain depends on whether you bought your property before or after 21 September 1999. This was the date when the federal government changed the rules for calculating a capital gain. With respect to property you purchased after 21 September 1999, the rules relating to calculating a capital gain are relatively straightforward, namely:

$ If you sell a property within 12 months of buying it and you make a capital gain, the entire gain you make on sale is liable to tax. This gain is called a non-discount capital gain.

$ If you sell a property more than 12 months after you buy it and you make a capital gain (which is generally the case), only 50 per cent of the capital gain you make on sale is liable to tax. The balance is exempt. This gain is called a discount capital gain.

Under the CGT provisions you will be considered to have sold your property at the time of the making of the contract, and not at the time of settlement. For example, if the contract of sale was entered into on 1 June 2010 and the settlement date was 1 August 2010, you will be deemed to have sold the property on 1 June 2010. Any capital gain you make is liable to tax in the financial year the property is sold. In the above example the capital gain would be returned in the 2009–10 financial year.

Case study: property bought after 21 September 1999

Four years ago Jason paid $300 000 for a rental property. At that time he paid $10 000 stamp duty and $500 legal costs. Jason sold the property today for $500 000. He paid $12 500 agent's commission to sell the property and $1000 legal costs. As Jason had purchased the property after 21 September 1999 and had owned it for more than 12 months he had made a discount capital gain. This means only 50 per cent of the capital gain is liable to tax. The balance is exempt. The capital gain that's liable to tax is calculated as follows:

Capital proceeds (sale price)		$500 000
Less:		
Cost base		
Purchase price	$300 000	
Stamp duty	$10 000	
Legal costs (buying)	$500	
Agent's commission	$12 500	
Legal costs (selling)	$1 000	$324 000
Capital gain		**$176 000**

As Jason had owned the property for more than 12 months and made a $176 000 capital gain on sale, he's only liable to pay tax on half the capital gain he made on sale, namely $88 000. The other half is exempt from tax. On the other hand, if Jason had sold the property within 12 months of buying it, the entire gain (namely, $176 000) would have been liable to tax.

Property bought between 20 September 1985 and 21 September 1999

There are two ways to calculate a capital gain in respect to property bought between 20 September 1985 and 21 September 1999. They are referred to as the discount method and indexation method. The good news here is you can select the method that will give you the better outcome. And that of course will be the one where you pay the least amount of tax. As many years have now elapsed since these new rules were introduced you'll most likely find the discount method will be the preferred option. Nowadays the indexation method is basically an academic exercise for tax students to ponder over!

Discount method

The discount method is exactly the same method that you use to calculate a capital gain today. At the time of sale, as you would have owned the property for more than 12 months, only half the capital gain you make is liable to tax. The other half is exempt.

Case study: discount method

On 17 October 1990 Margaret paid $150 000 for a residential property. At that time she paid $5000 stamp duty and $500 legal costs.

Case study *(cont'd)*: discount method

Margaret sold the property today for $600 000. She paid $14 000 agent's commission to sell the property and $500 legal costs. As Margaret purchased the property before 21 September 1999 and owned it for more than 12 months, under the discount method only 50 per cent of the capital gain is liable to tax. The balance is exempt. The capital gain that's liable to tax is calculated as follows:

Capital proceeds (sale price)		$600 000
Less:		
Cost base		
Purchase price	$150 000	
Stamp duty	$5 000	
Legal costs (buying)	$500	
Agent's commission	$14 000	
Legal costs (selling)	$500	$170 000
Capital gain		**$430 000**

In this case Margaret is liable to pay tax on half the capital gain she made on sale, namely $215 000.

Indexation method

If you use the indexation method you can adjust the purchase price and purchase costs for inflation. The consumer price index is used to make this adjustment. This is the index Australia uses to measure the rate of inflation. This was the way you calculated a capital gain in the good old days before the federal government changed the rules in September 1999. The bad news here is you can only do this adjustment for the period between the date you bought the property and 30 September 1999. So that's why with the passing of the years this method is now of academic interest only. Nevertheless, it doesn't do any harm to do the calculation. In this case Margaret will need to adjust the purchase price and purchase costs for inflation, for the period between the date she bought the property (17 October 1990) and 30 September 1999. The following formula is used to make this adjustment; the figures have been taken from table 13.1:

CPI at 30 September 1999 (123.4) ÷ CPI at date of purchase (106.0) = 1.164.

Because Margaret purchased the property and incurred all her purchase costs in the CPI quarter ending 31 December 1990, the CPI figure to do the above calculation is 106.0 (see table 13.1)

Capital proceeds (sale price)		$600 000
Less:		
Indexed cost base		
Purchase price ($150 000 × 1.164)	$174 600	
Stamp duty ($5000 × 1.164)	$5 820	
Legal costs (buying) ($500 × 1.164)	$582	
Agent's commission	$14 000	
Legal costs (selling)	$500	$195 502
Capital gain		**$404 498**

Under the indexation method the capital gain that's liable to tax is $404 498. It goes without saying that it would be more beneficial for Margaret to use the discount method as she'll only be liable to tax on $215 000.

Table 13.1: consumer price index

Year	31 March	30 June	30 September	31 December
1985	0	0	71.3	72.7
1986	74.4	75.6	77.6	79.8
1987	81.4	82.6	84.0	85.5
1988	87.0	88.5	90.2	92.0
1989	92.9	95.2	97.4	99.2
1990	100.9	102.5	103.3	**106.0**
1991	105.8	106.0	106.6	107.6

Table 13.1 *(cont'd)*: consumer price index

Year	31 March	30 June	30 September	31 December
1992	107.6	107.3	107.4	107.9
1993	108.9	109.3	109.8	110.0
1994	110.4	111.2	111.9	112.8
1995	114.7	116.2	117.6	118.5
1996	119.0	119.8	120.1	120.3
1997	120.5	120.2	119.7	120.0
1998	120.3	121.0	121.3	121.9
1999	121.8	122.3	**123.4**	

Source: Australian Bureau of Statistics

Capital loss

If the investment gods give you the thumbs down and you make a capital loss on sale of your property, the capital loss can only be deducted from a capital gain. While we're on this subject, a capital loss on a property transaction can be deducted from a capital gain you make from another asset class (for instance, a capital gain on shares). The only exception to the rule is you can't deduct it from a capital gain you make on a collectable. This is because capital losses on collectables can be deducted only from capital gains you make on collectables. If you haven't made any capital gains, the capital loss can be carried forward for an indefinite period and can be deducted from any capital gains you may make in the future. If you find yourself in this situation make sure you keep an accurate record of your capital losses. (Incidentally, if you're running a business and you incur a tax loss, the loss can be deducted from other assessable income you derive, for instance, salary and wages, business income and investment income.)

Case study: calculating a capital loss

Three years ago Andrew purchased a block of land for $250 000 and paid $7000 stamp duty and $500 legal costs. Andrew sold the block of land today for $220 000 and paid $5000 agent's commission and $500 legal fees to sell the land.

Capital proceeds (sale price)		$220 000
Less:		
Reduced cost base		
Purchase price	$250 000	
Stamp duty	$7 000	
Legal costs	$500	
Agent's commission	$5 000	
Legal costs	$500	$263 000
Capital loss		**$43 000**

In this case Andrew made a $43 000 capital loss. This capital loss can be applied against a current or future capital gain.

Non-deductible holding costs

Under Australian tax law if you buy a property for your personal use and enjoyment (for instance, a second home or a holiday house), non-deductible holding costs such as interest, land taxes, rates, insurance and repairs are not tax deductible. This is because the property doesn't derive income. The good news here is under the CGT provisions these costs can be added to the property's cost base and can be taken into account if you make a capital gain on sale. So make sure you keep an accurate record of these types of expenses. Incidentally, this tax concession is only available to non–income producing property you buy after 20 August 1991. There is also one more important condition and that is you can't take these costs into account if you happen to make a capital loss on sale.

Case study: non-deductible holding costs

Eight years ago Simon and Christine purchased a holiday house at a popular seaside resort for their personal use and enjoyment. The purchase price was $250 000 and the purchase costs were $10 000. During the time they owned the property they paid $40 000 non-deductible holding costs (such as interest, land tax, rates, insurance and repairs), which are not tax deductible. Simon and Christine sold the property today for $400 000 and the sale costs were $10 000. As the holiday house was purchased after 20 August 1991, and because they made a capital gain on the sale, they can deduct the $40 000 from the capital gain they made.

Capital proceeds (sale price)		$400 000
Less:		
Cost base		
Purchase price	$250 000	
Purchase costs	$10 000	
Holding costs	$40 000	
Sale costs	$10 000	$310 000
Capital gain		**$90 000**

In this case as the property was held for more than 12 months only $45 000 is liable to tax.

But if Simon and Christine had made a capital loss on sale, the $40 000 non-deductible holding costs could not be used to create or increase a capital loss. For example, if in this case the sale price was $200 000, the $40 000 costs cannot be used as it would have created or increased a capital loss.

Chapter 14

Home sweet home: using your residence to build wealth

For many investors buying a home could be the biggest decision they're ever likely to make. This is especially so if you have to borrow a truckload of money. The bad news here is you can't claim tax deductions (for instance, your interest payments) in respect to owning a main residence. But the good news is you're not up for capital gains tax if you make a capital gain on sale. In this chapter I chat about the different investment strategies you can consider if you own your main residence.

Your home is your castle

One of the great things about investing in a residential property is everyone needs a roof over their head. So there will always be a constant demand for a residential property if the price is right.

If you're thinking of buying a home I've got some good news and bad news. The bad news is any holding costs associated with owning a main residence (for instance, interest payments rates, insurance and repairs) are not tax deductible. This is because your property is not deriving assessable income. As a general rule, you should endeavour to pay off any home loan you've taken out as quickly as possible. But it's not all doom and gloom. Under Australian tax law your main residence is exempt from tax. This means you won't be up for any capital gains tax (CGT) if you make a capital gain on sale. So if you happen to be residing in a property that's constantly appreciating in value you'll probably be laughing all the way to the bank. This could prove a great way of building up your wealth if you can afford to buy a quality home in a much-sought-after suburb. Incidentally, under Australian tax law a main residence is defined as a place where you and your family normally reside, and can include up to two hectares of land that surrounds your property. While I'm on this subject, if you buy your next-door neighbour's property (for instance, a block of land), you can include it as part of your main residence. This is on the proviso that you don't breach the two hectares limit rule. But as they say in the classics, conditions apply. The newly acquired property must be used for your personal use and enjoyment (for instance, you put in a tennis court). And if you decide to sell your home down the track, you'll have to sell both holdings simultaneously to the new owner.

Handy tip

If you decide to subdivide your main residence and sell off part of the land, I've got some bad news. The main residence exemption benefit only applies if you sell your property in its entirety. So if you make a capital gain on the part that you sell off you're liable to pay CGT.

Government incentives

If you happen to be a first home buyer there are some handy government concessions to help you get started. For example, you could quality for a first home owner's grant. To get this grant you (and your partner) cannot have previously owned a property and you must live there for at least six months. If you satisfy these conditions you will receive a one-off payment amounting to $7000 to help you purchase an existing property or to build your own home. This grant is administered by various state and territory governments of Australia. At the time of writing it was announced the grant would only be available for properties valued up to a certain amount (see table 14.1). The federal government has also introduced first home saver accounts, where they'll contribute up to $850 per annum to help you save for a deposit. For more details you can visit the Australian Taxation Office website <www.ato.gov.au> and read fact sheet *First home saver accounts essentials*. Further, to help ease the pain of having to pay stamp duty—depending in which state or territory you reside—first home buyers may qualify for some stamp duty relief. For more details visit your local state or territory revenue office website.

Table 14.1: first home owner's grant — limits on value of properties

QLD	$1 million
NSW	$750 000
WA	$750 000
NT	$750 000
VIC	$600 000

Note: at the time of writing Tasmania, South Australia and the ACT had not made any announcement regarding this matter.

Temporary absent rule

One major concession available to home owners is the temporary absent rule. Under this rule if you leave your main residence and you lease it out, your property will continue to be exempt from CGT for up to six years while you're away. For example, you're temporarily posted overseas by your employer or move interstate and you lease your home while you're away. But the good news gets even better. If you don't lease your home while you're away (for example, you still have family occupying the property), your property will be exempt from CGT for the entire period you're away. To add icing to the cake, if you lease your property all your holding costs (particularly your interest payments) will become a tax deductible expense as your property is now deriving income. Now before you throw a party there is a 'teensy weensy' catch. And that is you can't own another main residence while you're away (it would be great if you could!). This is because under Australian tax law you can only own one main residence. In the meantime, if you do happen to buy another home you will have to nominate the one you intend claim the main residence exemption. The trick here is to choose the one that's going to make you the greatest capital gain in the long term! If you can't decide and you want to have a bob each way you can elect that 50 per cent of each property be treated as your main residence.

Now the news gets even better because the temporary absent rule can be used to your advantage. For example, if you're struggling to pay off the mortgage (or you're looking for a change of scenery) you could consider leasing. The rent you'll receive can help you service your loan repayments, and any interest, rates, insurance and repairs you incur will become a tax deductible expense! And if you can positive gear (meaning the rent more than covers your outlays), all the better. In the meantime, you'll need to find cheaper alternative accommodation (such as move in with mum if she'll have you back!). When I mentioned this at one of my wealth creation courses a woman became rather excited at the suggestion as she once resided at a caravan park! Before you jump at the idea it may be prudent for you to do some homework to see if doing this is a worthwhile exercise. Any additional revenue you make could go towards the cost of living elsewhere while you're away.

Rent and invest

There's a school of thought that goes along the lines that you should enter into a long lease in a location in which you're keen to reside and invest your surplus funds. The traditional way of buying a home is to take out a long-term mortgage (for instance, 20 years) and make regular repayments until the loan is repaid. Unfortunately, the substantial amount of interest payments plus rates, insurance and repairs you incur each year are not tax deductible. In contrast, if you lease (or you still live at home) you could invest your surplus funds. If you did this all the investment expenditure you incur is tax deductible. This could prove a lucrative way to quickly build up your wealth. Once you've accumulated sufficient funds from your investment activities you could consider buying your main residence at a later date.

Property bought before 20 September 1985

If you happen to own a main residence that you purchased before 20 September 1985 I've got some sensational news. This is especially the case if you're on the verge of retirement. Under Australian tax law any property purchased before this date is excluded from the CGT provisions. It doesn't make any difference whether it's your main residence or an investment property; they're all exempt from CGT. So if you're living in a pre-CGT property, you've effectively got an ace up your sleeve if you want to buy another property. For example, you're keen to buy a retirement home by the seaside or river. If you do this and move in, the property will be exempt from CGT given that it's now your *new* main residence! The great news here is you've now got two properties that will be exempt from CGT (namely your pre-CGT property and your new main residence). In the meantime, you could lease your first property to help supplement your lifestyle. But wait, there's more. If you change your mind down the track and you decide to live in your pre-CGT property again, under the temporary absent rule you can move out of your new main residence for an indefinite period provided you do not lease it out!

Buying an investment property

A major advantage of owning a main residence is you can use it as collateral to secure a loan to buy an investment property (or even a share portfolio). Under Australian tax law if the purpose of the loan is to buy an income-producing asset the expenses you incur are tax deductible (see chapter 13). The fact that you're using your main residence as collateral to secure the loan is irrelevant. Unfortunately, as mentioned previously this is not the case if the loan is to buy your main residence. In the meantime, the rent you receive from your investment property can help you service the loan repayments (see chapter 4, 'negative gearing'). If your investment property increases in value while you own it, you will be ahead. This could be worth considering if you can secure an interest-only loan. When the loan matures you could get another interest-only loan or you can sell your investment property and pocket any capital gain you make on sale. Alternatively, if your main residence and investment property are continually increasing in value you could consider taking out a further loan and buying another investment property (and continue the process of building wealth and loving it).

Handy tip

If you use your rental property as collateral to secure a loan to buy your main residence, the interest payments you incur are not tax deductible. This is because the purpose of the loan is to buy a non–income producing property (namely, your main residence).

The following case study illustrates how it's possible to build wealth using your main residence as collateral to buy an investment property. However, for this investment strategy to work in your favour two important conditions must be present:

$ the investment property you buy must increase in value

$ the rent you receive will predominantly cover your interest payments and holding costs. Any shortfall will be met from other income you derive (for instance, your salary and wages).

If either of these two conditions is not present there's a risk that you could get into financial differently. This is especially the case if interest rates were to rise significantly. So it's prudent that you seek professional advice before you contemplate this strategy.

Case study: buying an investment property

Christine has substantial equity in her own main residence, which is currently valued at $700 000. She approaches her local bank and puts her home up as collateral to secure a $400 000, 6 per cent interest-only loan to buy an investment property. The rent she'll receive will be $18 200 per annum ($350 per week) and the interest payments will be $24 000 per annum. As Christine's marginal rate of tax (plus Medicare levy) is 31.5 per cent, she calculates she'll need around $3000 (or $60 per week) to service the interest payments and rental costs each year, which of course are tax deductible.

Case study *(cont'd)*: buying an investment property

For more details see chapter 4, case study: negative gearing a property. In the meantime, if Christine's investment property doubles in value (for instance, within eight years) from $400 000 to $800 000 she will be miles ahead. When her interest-only loan matures she could consider taking out a new loan or sell the investment property, repay the $400 000 she borrowed and pocket a nice little earner. Alternatively, she could consider buying another investment property (or shares) and continue the process of building up her wealth.

Part III

Reaping the harvest: superannuation and retirement

The major dilemma you may face when it's time to hang up the pen or shovel and retire is whether you have managed to build up enough wealth to fund the next phase of your life. This is because the moment you retire the regular income you were deriving each fortnight ceases. From this moment onwards you're on your own. In part III I examine the pros and cons of building wealth in a superannuation fund and the various pension options you can buy with the super benefits you've accumulated over the years. I also chat about death and taxes and how your beneficiaries are taxed when your assets are distributed to them.

Chapter 15

Investing in superannuation

Superannuation is an investment vehicle to help you plan ahead to fund your retirement. If you're an employee the good news here is your employer must contribute 9 per cent of your gross pay into a complying super fund of your choice. There are also incentives to encourage low income earners and the self-employed to make a contribution as well. The money will be invested on your behalf and can't be touched until you retire. When that historic day arrives you can receive a pension, a lump sum payment or a combination of both. The good news gets even better because once you turn 60 all withdrawals are exempt from tax. In this chapter I chat about the different types of super funds and the various rules you'll need to follow if you want to make a contribution.

Superannuation — the icing on the cake

In an ideal world you should endeavour to accumulate wealth-creating assets within your superannuation fund as well as accumulating wealth-creating assets outside the super system. Speaking from personal experience, the amount you accumulate in your superannuation fund should be looked upon as a bonus — the icing on the cake — that will complement the investment portfolio you currently own. If you do this you will not be putting all your eggs in one basket. Although superannuation is a great way of building up your wealth, remember every dollar you put into super will be 'locked away' until you satisfy a condition of release such as when you retire. This can be a pain if you need the money now (for instance, to buy your home), and you have a large investment portfolio growing nicely in your super fund that you can't touch. But the great bit here is as you get close to retirement, you can transfer a substantial sum into super to boost your nest egg that you can access when it's time to hand up the pen or shovel (see figure 15.1 on page 208).

The test you had to have

We've all heard the old saying, 'out of sight, out of mind'. Well, no truer words have been spoken when it comes to superannuation. As superannuation is a long-term investment strategy, there's a tendency not to give it too much attention — especially if you've got a fair way to go before you retire. Now before you read on I'm going to spring a little surprise and give you an instant mini-test. This is to check whether you are consciously aware of your superannuation fund and how it's currently performing. So here are your questions — and no cheating!

1   Name your superannuation fund?

2   What is your current super fund balance?

3   What investment option (strategy) did you select and what does it mean?

4   What is the rate of return on your investment?

5   How did your super fund perform relative to other funds:

  ❑   under-performed?

  ❑   on a par?

  ❑   out-performed?

6   How much are the fees and costs you incur and why are you paying them?

7   Who are your preferred beneficiaries in the event of your death?

8   Did you take out any insurance cover?

9   What does 'preserved benefit' mean?

10 Are you accumulating enough capital to fund your retirement?

Now give yourself a mark out of 10. If you did extremely well, give yourself a pat on the back. If you did poorly it could suggest you're not paying enough attention to this important way of accumulating wealth. Remember, it's your money we are talking about here which will be used to fund your retirement.

Choice of superannuation fund

Under the superannuation provisions you have the right to choose your own superannuation fund to fund your retirement strategy. When you commence employment the first thing you'll have to do is set up a superannuation fund. This is because your employer has a statutory obligation to make a superannuation contribution on your behalf to your designated fund.

Figure 15.1: superannuation contributions

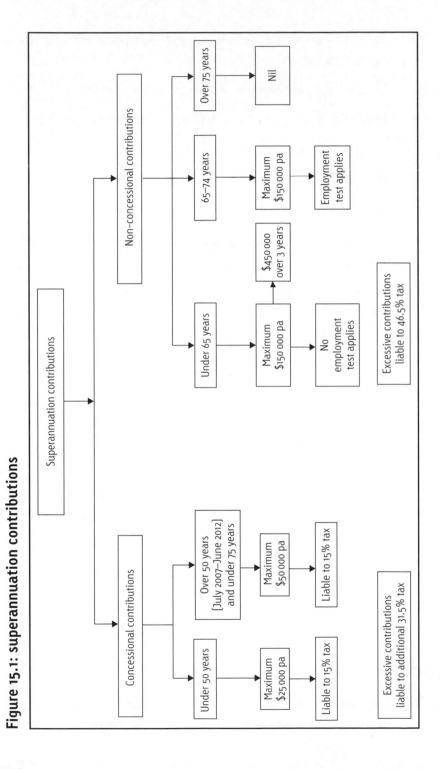

This amount is currently 9 per cent of your gross pay. So if you earn $1000 a week your employer will put in $90. If you haven't set a fund up your employer will choose a default fund for you. There are four types of superannuation funds you can contribute money to:

$ *Public sector funds.* These are funds that have been set up specifically for public servants. You'll generally find you have to be government employee if you want to make a contribution to these funds. So you may be ineligible to become a member.

$ *Retail funds.* These are funds that have been set up by Australia's leading financial institutions such as banks and life insurance companies. Anyone can make a contribution to these funds. The fees they charge to manage your money are normally based on a percentage of your fund balance. So it's important that you check whether you're getting value for your money — such as a better return on your investment — to justify these high costs. If you want more details you can visit the Association of Superannuation Funds of Australia (ASFA) website <www.superannuation.asn.au>.

$ *Industry funds.* These are funds that have been set up for specific industries (for instance, accountants, nurses and the police force). The great bit here is they are generally not-for-profit superannuation funds and anyone can become a member. The fees they charge to manage your money are generally much lower than those run by retail funds. Although this is great to know the ultimate test is their capacity to generate a good return on your investment. For more details you can visit the Industry Super Funds website <www.industrysuper.com>.

$ *Self managed superannuation funds (SMSF).* These are funds that are set up by individuals who would prefer to manage their own superannuation fund. It's generally considered you need about $250 000 to make this a viable option. Although running your own super fund may sound great, there are a number of stringent rules you'll need to comply with. There are also ongoing compliance costs associated with running a SMSF. I chat about this option in more detail in chapter 16.

Conditions of release: accessing your benefits

The following list sets out the main ways you can access your super-annuation fund benefits:

⇒ when you've reached your preservation age (see chapter 17)

⇒ when you turn 55 and elect to receive a transition to retirement pension (see chapter 17)

⇒ when you've reached 65 years of age

⇒ when you cease your current employment after age 60

⇒ severe financial hardship (conditions apply)

⇒ compassionate grounds

⇒ terminal illness

⇒ disablement or invalidity

⇒ temporary resident permanently departing Australia

⇒ death of member.

As superannuation funds are specifically set up to fund retirement strategies it's important that you keep a close eye on whether your nest egg is growing and the fees they charge you to manage your money. If you're dissatisfied with their results you have the right to rollover (transfer) your account balance to another superannuation fund provider.

Handy tip

When shopping around for a suitable super fund to grow your nest egg you should check out the following:

⇒ the fees and charges you'll incur

⇒ insurance options — particularly death and disability insurance

⇒ the diversity and investment options you'll be offered to fund your retirement [see chapter 6]

⇒ the various services and special features the super fund can offer its members.

What's so great about super?

The federal government has introduced a number of incentives to encourage you to make a contribution to a complying superannuation fund. By the way, the reason they're called complying funds is because they have agreed to be regulated under the *Superannuation Industry (Supervision) Act 1993.* All the major superannuation funds in Australia are regulated so this shouldn't be of any concern to you. So here are the benefits you can gain:

$ The investment earnings your fund makes are liable to a 15 per cent rate of tax as against your marginal tax rates (which can very between 0 per cent and 45 per cent).

$ If you're self-employed or substantially self-employed and you make a 'concessional contribution' the payment is tax deductible.

$ Employees can salary sacrifice part of their salary and wages (up to a certain amount) into a super fund and save on paying tax (more about this later).

$ There are some handy government incentives to encourage you to make a contribution if you are a low income earner.

$ Once you turn 55 years of age you can take a 'transition to retirement pension' while you're still working! I chat about this in more detail in chapter 17.

$ Pensions payable to members aged 55 to 59 will qualify for a 15 per cent tax offset. This means if you get a $45 000 pension (and this is your sole source of income) the 15 per cent tax offset will effectively reduce your personal tax bill to nil.

$ Pensions and lump sum payments payable to members after you turn 60 years of age are exempt from tax (see chapter 17).

$ Investment earnings to fund your pension options are exempt from tax.

Making a superannuation contribution

The great news here is that everyone under the age of 65 can make a contribution to a complying superannuation fund. However, there are rules to limit the amount you can put into a superannuation fund each financial year that you'll need to comply with. The rules associated with making a contribution will depend on whether:

$ you make a 'concessional contribution'

$ you make a 'non-concessional contribution'

$ you're under 65 years of age

$ you're over 65 years of age

$ you're an employee

$ you're self-employed (or substantially self-employed).

There are also federal government incentives to encourage low income earners to make a contribution to a superannuation fund. They are the 'government co-contribution scheme' and the 'spouse superannuation contributions tax offset'.

Concessional contributions

A concessional contribution is a contribution that qualifies for a tax deduction (see figure 15.1). Only employers and the self-employed (or substantially self-employed) can make a concessional contribution. When employers make a concessional contribution on behalf of their employees the super fund will deduct tax at the rate of 15 per cent from the payment. This will also be the case if you're self-employed (or substantially self-employed). So every time your employer makes a contribution on your behalf you'll find 15 per cent tax has been withheld. For example, if your employer makes a $10 000 concessional contribution on your behalf, $1500 tax will be deducted which means you will only have $8500 to invest. Under Australian tax law the maximum concessional contribution that'll qualify for a tax deduction will depend on your age at the time the payment is made, namely:

$ $25 000 (indexed) per annum if you're under 50 years of age

$ $50 000 per annum if you're over 50 years of age between July 2007 and June 2012 and under 75 years of age.

You will be up for additional tax if you breach these rules (see figure 15.1). Nevertheless, if you want to put more funds into your superannuation fund you have the option to make a non-concessional contribution (see overleaf).

Non-concessional contributions

A non-concessional contribution is a contribution that does not qualify for a tax deduction (see figure 15.1). Since this payment is a capital contribution it won't be liable to tax. As employees can't claim a tax deduction they can only make non-concessional contributions. For example, if an employee makes a $10 000 non-concessional contribution no tax is payable—which means they'll have $10 000 to invest. Under Australian tax law if you're under 65 years of age you can contribute up to a maximum $150 000 (indexed) non-concessional contributions each year. Alternatively, you can make a $450 000 non-concessional contribution over a three-year period (provided you're under 65 years at the time the payment is made). However, you're liable to pay additional tax if you exceed these limits (see figure 15.1). By the way, it's possible for you to make a $600 000 non-concessional contribution over a two-month period; for example, you can make a $150 000 contribution just before the end of the financial year (for instance, in June), and a further $450 000 at the beginning of the next financial year (for instance, in July) (see chapter 16 'case study: comparing different investment options'). If you do this you can't make another contribution for the next three years. This could be a great way of injecting a substantial sum to boost your superannuation fund nest egg, especially as you get close to your retirement age.

Under 65 years of age

There is nothing to stop you from making a non-concessional contribution to a complying superannuation fund if you're under 65 years of age. However, if you plan to do this, make sure you don't exceed the contribution limits discussed in the previous section.

Over 65 years of age

If you are aged between 65 and 74 years and you want to make a non-concessional contribution, you will need to satisfy an employment test. To satisfy this test you'll need to work a minimum 40 hours over a 30-day consecutive period during the financial year. Once you turn 65 years of age you can only contribute up to a maximum of $150 000 non-concessional contributions. The ability to contribute $450 000 will no longer be available to you. Unfortunately, once you turn 75 years of age you can no longer make a non-concessional contribution to a complying superannuation fund.

Employee

As mentioned previously, employers have a statutory obligation to make a concessional contribution on your behalf. This amount is 9 per cent of your gross pay. For example, if you earn $60 000 per annum your employer must make a $5400 contribution to your super fund ($60 000 × 9 per cent). To help build the nest egg employees can also make additional contributions under a 'salary sacrifice' arrangement, where additional superannuation contributions can be deducted from your gross pay. For example, you ask your employer to make a further $10 000 superannuation contribution. If you do this your taxable income will reduce from $60 000 to $50 000. And the $10 000 will be taxed at the rate of 15 per cent by the super fund, rather than at your marginal tax rates (30 per cent) if you did not salary sacrifice. You will effectively save $1500 in tax! But the catch here is you can't access these funds until you satisfy a condition of release (see chapter 16). However, employees cannot claim a tax deduction in respect to the additional amount they contribute. Both the employer and employee portion cannot exceed $25 000 per annum if you're under

50 years of age or $50 000 if you're over 50 between July 2007 and June 2012 and under 75 years of age (see figure 15.1).

Self-employed (or substantially self-employed)

If a self-employed or substantially self-employed person makes a concessional contribution to a complying superannuation fund the contribution is a tax deductible expense. These contributions are taxed in the super fund at the rate of 15 per cent. A self-employed person is someone who receives no superannuation support. Conversely, a substantially self-employed person is a person who derives less than 10 per cent of their assessable income from a superannuation-supported source; for example, you're under 65 years and not in full-time employment (for instance, you're a retiree or parent looking after a small child). As is the case with employers and employees, the maximum concessional contribution that will qualify for a tax deduction is $25 000 if you are under 50 years of age or $50 000 if you're over 50 years of age between July 2007 and June 2012.

Government co-contribution

If you make a non-concessional contribution to your super-annuation fund, the federal government will also make a contribution on your behalf to help build your superannuation fund balance. But as they say in the classics, conditions apply. At the time of writing if your total assessable income is less than $31 920 (indexed) and you make a $1000 non-concessional contribution, the federal government will also make a contribution as set out in table 15.1 with no strings attached. The amount the government contributes will begin to diminish as you earn more money and will cease once you earn more than $61 920 (indexed).

Table 15.1: superannuation co-contribution scheme (government contribution for $1000 non-concessional member contribution)

Financial year	Amount	Percentage contributed
2009–10	$1000	100%
2010–11	$1000	100%
2011–12	$1000	100%
2012–13	$1250	125%
2013–14	$1250	125%
2014–15	$1500	150%

Spouse contribution tax offset

If your spouse's assessable income is $10 800 or less, you could qualify for a $540 tax offset (18% × $10 800) if you make a $3000 contribution to your spouse's complying superannuation fund or a retirement savings account operated by an 'approved financial institution'. The tax offset is reduced if your spouse earns more than $10 800 and will reduce to nil once your spouse earns more than $13 800.

Member benefit statements

Your super fund will normally issue two member benefit statements each year setting out the following details:

⇒ *personal details:* name and address, member number, date you joined the fund, date of birth and your tax file number

⇒ *investment options:* for instance, cash, capital stable, balanced, growth, equity growth or property

⇒ *your insurance benefits:* death and disability and/or income protection cover

---

Member benefit statements *(cont'd)*

⇛ *opening and closing balances:* you'll be hoping the closing balance will be more than the opening balance!

⇛ *amounts added to account:* for instance, contributions, rollover and transfers, and investment returns

⇛ *amounts deducted from account:* for instance, taxes, fees, insurance premiums, withdrawals

⇛ *transaction history:* providing a summary of all contributions

⇛ *Description of your entitlements:*

◻ preserved benefit: being the balance in your super fund that you can access when you reach your preservation age and retire

◻ restricted non-preserved: being funds you can access when you retire or you satisfy a condition of release (for instance, you terminate your current employment)

◻ unrestricted non-preserved: being funds you can access immediately

⇛ *beneficiary details:* nominated beneficiary to receive your benefits in the event of your death.

Chapter 16

Self managed superannuation funds

So you've received your member benefit statement from your super fund, and you're not impressed with how they're managing your money or you consider the fees are too high. If you think you can do a better job, setting up a self managed superannuation fund may be the way to go. Before you get excited there are stringent rules you'll need to follow if you want to run the show yourself. In this chapter I chat about the pros and cons of setting up and managing your own super fund.

The good and the bad

Setting up a self managed superannuation fund (SMSF) is ideal if you run your own business, and/or you're a mature investor (for instance, you're in your mid 40s) with accumulated funds in excess of $250 000 — it's generally accepted you'll need this ball-park amount to make it cost effective. When you set up a SMSF you must make an election within 60 days to be regulated by the Australian Taxation Office (ATO). You'll have to do this in order to become a complying superannuation fund. This is because if you want to gain all the benefits from running your own super fund you must comply with all the ATO rules and regulations. For instance, you can only have a maximum of four members and all the members must be trustees of your fund. The members normally have a close family relationship (for instance, husband and wife), or are business partners or friends.

Handy tip

The ATO has issued the following publications to help you understand and comply with all the rules and regulations associated with running a SMSF:

⇒ *Setting up a Self Managed Super Fund*

⇒ *Our Role in Regulating Self Managed Superannuation Funds*

⇒ *The SMSF News*

⇒ *Self Managed Superannuation Funds — Investment Strategy and Investment Restrictions*

If you want a copy of these publications you can contact the ATO directly or you can visit its website ‹www.ato.gov.au›.

There are many reasons why running your own superannuation fund may be worth doing:

$ *Total control.* You will be in total control of your superannuation fund assets, and you will make all the decisions regarding the administration of your super fund. This may sound great. But the ATO expects all members to be fully aware of and comply with all the stringent rules and regulations associated with running a SMSF.

$ *Investment strategy.* You can select your own investment strategy to help grow your wealth to fund your retirement. A major rule here that you've got to comply with is to formulate an investment strategy setting out how you intend to invest your money. More about this later.

$ *Make contributions.* You can make superannuation contributions to your SMSF (both concessional and non-concessional contributions). For more details see chapter 15.

$ *Listed securities.* One great thing about running your own super fund is you can transfer your 'listed securities' (such as your personal share portfolio) and continue investing within your super fund. However, under Australian tax law if you do this you'll be effectively selling your investment assets to your super fund, and you could be up for capital gains tax. Also keep in mind you won't be able to access your benefits until you satisfy a condition of release and retire.

$ *Business real property.* If you run your own business it's also possible for your super fund to own your business premises and lease it back to you. If you plan to do this your super fund must charge you a commercial rate of rent. If you want more details the Tax Office has released the guidelines, *What constitutes business real property in respect to SMSF.*

$ *Life insurance.* If you incur life insurance payments in your super fund the payments are tax deductible. This is not the case if you have a life insurance policy outside the super system.

$ *Administration duties.* You can outsource all your administration duties to superannuation specialists and the expenses the super fund incurs are tax deductible.

$ *Estate planning.* You can instigate estate-planning strategies and you can nominate beneficiaries who stand to benefit in the event of your death (see chapter 18).

$ *Pension payments.* Once you satisfy a condition of release (such as when you retire), you can convert your superannuation fund from an accumulation fund into a pension fund and pay yourself a pension (see chapter 17).

However, before you set up your SMSF you'll need to weigh up whether you have the necessary skills (and personal commitment) to manage your own investment strategies. This means you must manage your investments prudently and be able to assess risk and investment options. A key test here is whether you are capable of outperforming the professionally managed super funds. You may incur a number of costs such as:

$ audit fees to audit your super fund — this must be done annually

$ accounting fees

$ financial advice fees

$ tax agent fees

$ compliance costs (such as a $150 supervisory levy).

If you outsource the administration work associated with running a SMSF, the amount you'll be charged will depend on how complicated your superannuation structure is. So you may need to shop around for the best deal if you don't want to do the work yourself.

The rules you have to follow

Once you've elected to be regulated there are a number of stringent rules and regulations that you'll need to follow. If you fail to comply your super fund will become a non-complying superannuation fund. This means you'll lose all the benefits associated with running a super fund, and you'll be liable to pay tax at the rate of 45 per cent (rather than 15 per cent if you're a complying super fund). To ensure your fund is a complying fund, you must appoint an approved auditor each year to check that you're not contravening any provisions. If you do breach any rules the auditor must report the contraventions to the Tax Office. The key rules and regulations you'll need to comply with are set out here:

$ *Sole purpose test.* Your superannuation fund must be set up for the sole purpose of providing benefits to members upon retirement, and to provide benefits to dependants in the event of a member's death. This means you cannot gain any benefits from your super fund until you satisfy a condition of release and retire, for example:

   □ you cannot reside in a property that is owned by your super fund

   □ you cannot enjoy a direct or indirect benefit from your super fund's investments; for example, display art your super fund owns in your place of residence or wear jewellery your super fund may own as an investment asset

   □ you can not use or benefit from discount cards companies such as those you're investing in may offer their shareholders (as you'll be considered to be gaining a benefit before retirement)

   □ you cannot use your fund's assets as a guarantee to secure a personal loan.

$ *Separation of assets.* You must keep your personal investments separated from your superannuation fund's investments. This means you'll need to maintain a separate superannuation fund bank account to record all your super fund's financial transactions. Keep in mind your superannuation fund's investments do not belong to you until you satisfy a condition of release. (For more details you should read tax determination ID 2002/976 *Keeping assets of a self managed superannuation fund separate from assets of other parties.*)

$ *Investment strategy.* Your SMSF must formulate an investment strategy regarding your investment holdings, and all your investment decisions must be done on a commercial basis. Your investment strategy must be in writing setting out the following important information:

◻ your objectives; for example, to achieve a rate of return that is 5 per cent above the annual inflation rate

◻ the mix of investments you intend to hold to achieve your objectives; for example, part cash, shares, property and managed funds

◻ the risks involved in respect to the investments you intend to hold to achieve your objectives

◻ the likely return on your investment; for example, 10 per cent per annum

◻ that you'll have sufficient funds on hand to discharge any current or prospective liabilities; this could become a problem if your super fund's major asset is a property that cannot be readily converted into cash.

You will need to review your investment strategy at regular intervals and make any appropriate adjustments considered necessary.

You'll also need to keep proper records to verify the existence of your fund's investments at the time your super fund is audited. Further, your fund must keep accurate valuations of your super fund's investments (for instance, at market value). Members can elect to have a 'pooled investment strategy' where all member funds are pooled, or an individual investment strategy where each individual member will choose their own investment strategy. By the way, if you have a pooled investment strategy you will need to know how the fund's earnings are to be allocated to each member's account and when this should take place. As this can be a complex exercise you should seek professional advice if you're not sure what to do.

$ *Borrowings.* As a general rule your superannuation fund cannot borrow money to help build up superannuation fund assets, nor can it lend money to you. But there is one major exception. A SMSF can borrow using an 'instalment warrant' to fund the purchase of investment assets such as a residential property, commercial property, listed securities and artwork. There are strict rules that you'll need to follow if you want to use an instalment warrant to help grow your investment holdings. If you need additional information the Tax Office has issued a publication titled *Instalment warrants and super funds—questions and answers* as well as Taxpayer Alert TA 2008/5 *Certain borrowings by self managed superannuation funds.*

$ *Keep proper records.* You must maintain a record of your 'minutes of trustee meetings'. You'll also have to keep separate member accounts, determine each financial year the earnings of the super fund and notify members of their account balances at regular intervals (for instance, every six months).

Handy tip

The Tax Office has issued the following interpretative decisions (ID) and newsletter relating to a super fund's inability to acquire assets from related parties:

⇒ ID 2002/381 *Investment and sole purpose: discount card share*

⇒ ID 2002/732 *Acquisition of residential property from members*

⇒ ID 2003/807 *Related party acquisitions: unit in short-term accommodation complex*

⇒ ID 2003/1127 *Acquisition of collectable notes and coins from related party*

⇒ ID 2004/92 *Acquisition of residential property from members*

⇒ *SMSF Newsletter* edition 1 relating to investing in 'wine, vintage cars, artwork and super'.

Taxing your self managed super fund

At the end of each financial year you'll need to lodge a super-annuation fund tax return by 31 October disclosing the fund's taxable income. Incidentally, the fund's taxable income is a combination of concessional contributions from members plus investment earnings (such as interest, dividends, rent and capital gains) less allowable deductions. At the time of lodgement your fund will be liable to pay a $150 supervisory levy. And don't forget you can't lodge a super fund tax return until your accounts have been audited, and your auditor gives you the thumbs up. The investment income your super fund derives is liable to tax at the rate of 15 per cent. If your super fund makes a capital gain on sale of investment assets, only two-thirds of the gain is liable to tax if the investment assets were held for more than 12 months. With respect to allowable deductions the Australian Taxation Office has issued Taxation Ruling TR 93/17 that provides comprehensive details about the types of expenditure a self managed superannuation fund can claim. The main ones are listed here:

$ accountancy fees

$ actuarial fees

$ audit fees

$ compliance costs

$ cost of amending trust deed

$ death and disability premiums

$ insurance payments

$ investment advice

$ legal costs

$ tax agent fees.

If your super fund were to derive dividend franking credits the amount will be deducted from the tax payable. The following case study illustrates how a complying superannuation fund is taxed.

Case study: taxing your super fund

At the end of the financial year the financial accounts of Crabtree complying superannuation fund provided the following information:

Concessional contributions from members	$10 000
Dividends fully franked	$14 000
Dividend franking credits	$6 000
Interest credited	$2 000
Capital gains on investments held for less than 12 months	$4 000
Allowable deductions (audit and accounting fees)	$2 000

Case study *(cont'd)*: taxing your super fund

This is how the superannuation fund is taxed:

Taxable income

Concessional contributions from members	$10 000
Dividends fully franked	$14 000
Dividend franking credits	$6 000
Interest credited	$2 000
Capital gains on sale of investments	$4 000
Total income	**$36 000**

Less:

Deductions	$2 000
Taxable income	**$34 000**

Calculating tax payable/tax refund

Tax payable [$34 000 × 15%]	$5 100

Less:

Dividend franking credits	$6 000
Net tax refund	**$900**

As the dividend franking credits exceeded the tax payable Crabtree complying superannuation fund will get a $900 tax refund.

Comparing different investment options

The following case study compares the different investment options and the return on your investment (after tax) if you decide to invest your capital in a self managed superannuation fund or outside the superannuation system, and more particularly in shares, property and term deposits.

Case study: comparing different investment options

John, who will turn 60 years of age on 1 June, has $600000 to invest. He has just set up a self managed super fund and is contemplating the following options.

Option 1: invest in a self managed super fund

As John has $600000 to invest and is under 65 years of age, he will need to make two contributions. Otherwise he'll breach the superannuation provisions. So he makes a $150000 contribution before the end of the financial year and a further $450000 at the beginning of the next financial year.

Investment	$600000
Investment allocation	Shares (paying fully franked dividends)
Earnings rate	5%
Annual earnings	$42857 (consisting of dividends and franking credits)
Tax payable	Nil
Net earnings	**$42857**

Comments:

⇒   As John is 60 years of age he will pay no tax on the net earnings.

⇒   John can withdraw a $42857 tax-free pension which will be excluded from his assessable income.

⇒   Any capital growth is tax free.

⇒   John can earn a further $16000 before he's liable to pay tax (per 2010–11 tax rates).

Option 2: invest in shares (outside super)

Investment	$600000
Investment allocation	Shares (paying fully franked dividends)
Earnings rate	5%
Dividends	$30000
Franking credits	$12857

Case study *(cont'd)*: comparing different investment options

Less:

Tax payable	$6 063
Tax refund	$6 794
Net earnings	**$36 794**

Comments:

⇒   If John invests the funds outside the super fund he will be $6063 worse off.

⇒   Any capital growth is liable to capital gains tax.

⇒   John would be better off purchasing his share portfolio in his self managed super fund.

Option 3: invest in property (outside super)

Investment	$600 000
Investment allocation	Property
Gross rental yield	4%
Rental costs	$3 000
Gross rent	$24 000

Less:

Rental costs	$3 000
Tax payable	$1 065
Net earnings	**$19 935**

Comments:

⇒   Any capital growth is liable to capital gains tax on sale.

⇒   If the property was purchased in the super fund the return would have been $21 000 as no tax is payable.

Option 4: invest in a term deposit (outside super)

Investment	$600 000
Investment allocation	Term deposit
Interest rate	5%
Interest derived	$30 000

Less:

Tax payable $2 550

Net earnings **$27 450**

Comments:

⇛ No capital growth.

⇛ If the term deposit was invested in the self managed super fund the return would have been $30 000 as no tax is payable.

Chapter 17

Receiving a pension

When you come to think about it, the day you retire is similar to sitting for an important exam to test your knowledge. The exam in this case is whether you have managed to accumulate enough capital to live comfortably in retirement. When the federal government introduced compulsory superannuation in the early 1990s it was sending a clear message that you've got to fund your own retirement. Relying on government handouts is no longer a viable option unless you're on the breadline. In this chapter I chat about the various superannuation pensions you can buy using the super fund benefits you've accumulated over the years.

Condition of release

Investing in superannuation is a great way of accumulating wealth that you can access once you've reached your preservation age and satisfy a condition of release. The most common condition is when you retire. In the meantime, during the 'accumulation phase' your earnings will be taxed at the rate of 15 per cent. And if you receive dividend franking credits your tax bill will be reduced (see chapter 16 'case study: taxing your superannuation fund'). Under Australian tax law your preservation age will depend on the date you were born; for example, if you were born before 1960 you can access your funds once you reach 55 years of age, and if you were born after 1964 you'll have to wait until you turn 60 (see table 17.1).

Table 17.1: preservation age

Date of birth	Preservation age
Before 1 July 1960	55 years
1 July 1960–30 June 1961	56 years
1 July 1961–30 June 1962	57 years
1 July 1962–30 June 1963	58 years
1 July 1963–30 June 1964	59 years
After 30 June 1964	60 years

Taxing your pension

The great news about buying a superannuation pension with your accumulated funds is once you turn 60 years of age, all pension payments and cash withdrawals are exempt from tax. As this pension doesn't have to be declared in your individual tax return, you can effectively earn a further $16000 before you're liable to pay tax. But wait, there's more. The earnings from the investments to fund your pension payments are also exempt from tax. If you're between 55 and 59 years of age and you decide to retire, the taxable component of your pension will be taxed at your marginal rate plus a Medicare levy. To help ease the pain you can claim a 15 per cent tax offset. For example, if your pension is $40 000, you can claim a $6000 tax offset (which is 15% of $40 000) from the net tax payable (see figure 17.1). There is, however, an exception to the rule if you happen to be a government employee. As certain government super funds don't pay tax, the taxable component of your pension payments is liable to tax at your marginal rates plus a Medicare levy. The good news is once you turn 60 years of age you can claim a 10 per cent tax offset (see figure 17.1, overleaf).

Buying a pension

There are three different types of superannuation pensions you can purchase with your accumulated superannuation fund benefits. Each pension option will have certain features that may appeal to you. The pension you'll select will ultimately depend on your personal preference and lifestyle needs. They are called:

$ transition to retirement pension

$ non–account based pension (or life pension)

$ account-based pension (or allocated pension).

Handy tip

One major option you have up your sleeve if you happen to own your main residence Is to sell and downsize. This could be very beneficial if your home has increased substantially in value, and you're looking for additional funds to supplement your retirement nest egg. As your main residence is an exempt CGT asset any capital gain you make on the sale won't be taxed. You could then buy a cheaper residential home or apartment with the proceeds and invest the balance in a complying superannuation fund. And of course if you're over 60 years of age the additional pension you'll receive will be tax free.

Figure 17.1: superannuation pensions

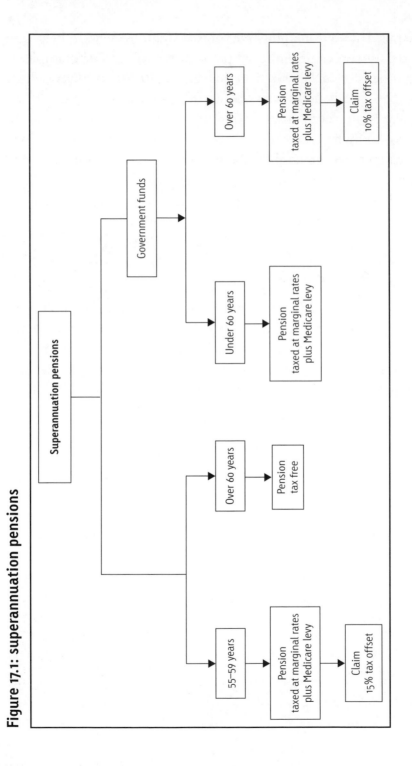

Transition to retirement pension

A transition to retirement pension will appeal to members who would like to receive a superannuation pension and still remain gainfully employed on either a full-time or part-time basis. There are three important conditions you'll need to comply with if you would like to receive this type of pension:

$ You must be at least 55 years of age at the time you apply for the pension.

$ You must elect to receive a non-commutable pension. This means while you're in receipt of the pension you can't convert the pension back into a lump sum payment until you reach 65 years of age or you decide to retire.

$ The amount you can withdraw must fall between 4 per cent and 10 per cent of the balance in your super fund account. For example, if you have $250 000 in your super fund account, you can withdraw a pension that falls between $10 000 and $25 000 per annum.

If you're between 55 and 59 years of age at the time you receive a transition to retirement pension you will qualify for a 15 per cent tax offset. Further, any investment income your superannuation fund derives during the pension phase to fund your pension payments will also be exempt from tax.

The great thing about this arrangement is you can continue working while you get the pension. It also gives you the opportunity to increase your cash flow to supplement any salary and wages you're currently earning. By the way, if you're still working once you turn 55 years of age you could receive a $500 mature age tax offset. In the meantime, you have the option to make further contributions to your superannuation fund that you can access when you finally decide to retire (see chapter 15, figure 15.1).

Case study: transition to retirement pension

Cynthia is 58 years of age and has a $400 000 balance in her complying superannuation fund account. She likes the idea that she can get a pension and still keep working. The pension she'll receive will help supplement the salary and wages she's currently earning. According to the rules, Cynthia will need to take a pension that falls between $16 000 per annum (4 per cent of $400 000) and $40 000 per annum (10 per cent of $400 000). This year she has elected to receive $20 000. This pension is liable to tax at her marginal rates, and because she's under 60 years of age, she'll qualify for a $3000 tax offset (15 per cent of $20 000). The great news here is once she turns 60 years of age, the pension will be entirely exempt from tax and excluded from her assessable income. The investment earnings her super fund derives to fund her pension payments will also be exempt from tax. In the meantime, Cynthia has decided to make a $5000 salary sacrifice contribution into her super fund that she can access when she decides to permanently retire.

Non–account based pension

If you want a non–account based pension you will use your accumulated superannuation fund account balance to buy this pension. Non–account based pensions are normally lifetime pensions. This means you will be assured of getting this pension for the rest of your life. The great news with this type of pension option is if the investments used to fund your pension were to fall in value the superannuation fund provider bears all the risk. If you're between 55 and 59 years of age at the time you get the pension you'll qualify for a 15 per cent tax offset. And of course once you turn 60 years of age the pension will be exempt from tax and excluded from your assessable income.

Although this pension may sound great if you're looking for this type of security, it will come at a cost. This is because you can only increase your pension payments each year to counter the impact of inflation, and you will not be allowed to withdraw any additional funds. Worse still, if you change your mind down the track you will not be allowed to commute (change) your pension back into a lump sum payment. This may not be a viable pension option to consider if you're in a poor state of health at the time you take the pension. There's a risk if you die shortly after the pension commences that your beneficiaries will not get any benefits from this pension arrangement. So before you commit yourself you should seek professional advice to see whether this pension is right for you.

Handy tip

A self managed superannuation fund cannot pay its members a non–account based pension.

Case study: non–account based pension

Kevin is 60 years of age and has an $800 000 balance in his accumulated superannuation fund account balance. Being in good health he likes the idea of receiving a guaranteed pension for the rest of his life. In exchange for his lump sum payment he will receive a $40 000 pension payable on a fortnightly basis. The amount he'll receive can only be adjusted annually to counter the impact of inflation. As Kevin is 60 years of age the pension is exempt from tax and excluded from his assessable income. Any investment income his superannuation fund derives during the pension phase to fund the pension payments will also be exempt from tax. A major risk here is if Kevin were to die shortly after he purchases the pension his beneficiaries may not qualify for any benefits.

Account-based pension

Account-based pensions (commonly known as allocated pensions) have a number of features that may appeal to you. Under this pension option your accumulated superannuation fund benefits will be invested on your behalf and the funds will be used to pay you an annual pension. If you're between 55 and 59 years of age the pension will qualify for a 15 per cent tax offset. For example, if you receive a $40 000 pension you will qualify for a $6000 tax offset ($6000 × 15 per cent). But once you turn 60 years of age the entire pension is exempt from tax and excluded from your assessable income. Any investment income your superannuation fund derives during the pension phase to fund the pension payments will also be exempt from tax.

The great bit here is you can vary your pension payments each year and the pension will continue to be paid until all your funds are diminished. The pension is recalculated at the beginning of each financial year and the amount you'll receive will depend on how much you have in your account. A major benefit with this pension option is there are no maximum withdrawal limits. This means you can withdraw as much as you like, and you can commute (change) your pension back into a lump sum payment. To add icing to the cake you can terminate the pension whenever you wish to do so. And your pension can be paid to your spouse in the event of your death or the balance can be paid to your estate.

But as they say in the classics, conditions apply. The pension must be paid to you annually, and you must receive a prescribed minimum which can vary between 4 per cent and 14 per cent of your account balance. For example, if you're under 65 years of age you must withdraw at least 4 per cent of your account balance, and 14 per cent if you're 95 years and over (see table 17.2). A major risk with this pension option is your funds can quickly reduce if the investments you choose to fund your pension fall in value. So it's important that you invest your money prudently. Further, once you set up the pension fund you cannot make any further contributions. If you have additional funds, you can either set up another pension fund or terminate the pension fund you currently have and start again.

Table 17.2: minimum superannuation pension payments

Age	Minimum pension withdrawals from account (per cent)
Under 65	4
65–74	5
75–79	6
80–84	7
85–89	9
90–94	11
95 and over	14

Case study: account-based pension

Anna is 58 years of age and has a $750 000 balance in her accumulated superannuation fund account. She has elected to receive an account-based pension (allocated pension) as she likes the various features this pension can offer her. Accounting to table 17.2 the minimum pension Anna can get is $30 000 per annum, but she has the option to withdraw more if necessary. This financial year she has elected to receive a $40 000 pension. As Anna is between 55 and 59 years of age the pension is liable to tax at her marginal rates, but she will qualify for a $6000 tax offset (being 15 per cent of $40 000). Once Anna turns 60 years of age the entire pension is exempt from tax and excluded from her assessable income. Any investment income her superannuation fund derives during the pension phase to fund her pension is also exempt from tax.

Old age pension

Although the federal government has incentives in place to encourage you to fund your own retirement, if you're unable to do so or you have insufficient funds, you could be eligible for the old age pension. To qualify for this pension you will need to satisfy an income test and asset test. These tests check whether the amount of income you derive each year and the amount of assets you own are within acceptable statutory limits. Otherwise you could miss out.

If you want to know whether you qualify for a full or part pension you can contact Centrelink directly or visit its website ‹www.centrelink. gov.au›. A qualified financial planner can do this for you, and/or advise you as to what you may need to do to qualify for this pension. Further, depending on your age (for instance, you're 65 years of age), the amount you earn each year, and whether you're single or a couple, you could qualify for a senior Australians tax offset. This tax offset is applied against the tax you're liable to pay on the taxable income you derive each year. For more details visit the Australian Taxation Office website ‹www.ato.gov.au› and read the fact sheet *What is the senior Australians tax offset?*

Chapter 18

Parting is such sweet sorrow: death and taxes

During your lifetime it's quite possible for you to accumulate many assets. The bad news is you can't take them with you when you die. So it's important that you make provisions as to who should get them before you go to the big retirement house in the sky. The good news is there are no death taxes or an inheritance tax to worry about. Before your beneficiaries jump for joy, the bad news is they could become personally liable to pay capital gains tax if they sell them down the track. In this chapter I chat about the two things you can't escape from, death and taxes.

Your last will and testament

Your last will and testament is a legal document that's normally prepared by a solicitor. It will set out your final instructions as to who should get your assets in the event of your death. Although there are no rules to prevent you from distributing them to specific beneficiaries, when you take the CGT provisions into account, it could influence your decision as to who should get certain assets you currently own.

> **Handy tip**
>
> In the event of your death the executor of your estate will take control of your financial affairs, until all your assets have been distributed to your beneficiaries in accordance with your instructions. In the meantime, your executor is required to lodge a tax return disclosing income you derived up to the date of your death, and a trust return in respect of any income you derive after your death (for instance, interest, dividends and rent from your investment portfolio).

Death and capital gains tax

Under the CGT provisions a liability to CGT arises when there is a disposal of a CGT asset (for instance, your share portfolio and real estate). As death does not constitute a disposal, there are no CGT issues to worry about at the time the beneficiaries inherit them. It's only when the beneficiaries sell them that a CGT issue will arise. The amount of any potential CGT payable will depend on whether the deceased bought the CGT assets before or after 20 September 1985. This was the date when the CGT provisions were first introduced in Australia. To complicate matters even further there are certain CGT assets that are specifically exempt from tax.

Before 20 September 1985

Any assets acquired before 20 September 1985 are specifically excluded from the CGT provisions. When these assets are distributed to your beneficiaries, they will be deemed to have been acquired on the date of death at their *market value*. This means any increase in value from the date the deceased bought them to the date of death is ignored. For example, if a deceased paid $100 000 for an investment property in 1984 and dies today, the beneficiary will be deemed to have acquired the property on the date of death at its market value. If the market value was $700 000, then this will be the beneficiary's cost base. So any increase in value up to this point in time (in this case, $600 000) is ignored. However, the beneficiary will be personally liable to pay tax on any subsequent increase in value from this point onwards. For example, if the beneficiary were to sell the property two years later for $900 000, the beneficiary is personally liable to pay tax on any increase in value that's above $700 000. In this case this will be $200 000. As the CGT asset was held for more than 12 months only 50 per cent of the capital gain is taxable (see chapter 9, figure 9.1). Incidentally, the 12 months ownership rule commences from the date the deceased acquired the property.

After 19 September 1985

With respect to assets acquired on or after 20 September 1985 the rules are somewhat nasty. If you inherit these assets you will be deemed to have acquired them on the date of death at the value the deceased originally acquired them (namely the deceased's cost base). This means the beneficiary is liable to pay CGT on any increase in value during the time the deceased owned the asset, plus any further increase in value during the time the beneficiary owned it. For example, if the deceased paid $100 000 for an investment property in 1986 and dies today, the beneficiary will be deemed to have acquired the property on the date of death at that value (namely $100 000). If the property continues to increase in value the beneficiary is liable to pay tax on the increase in value during the time the deceased owned it, plus any further increase in value during the time the beneficiary owned it. For example, if the beneficiary were to sell the property two years later for $900 000, the capital gain on sale is $800 000 (being the difference between the sale price and the deceased's cost base) (double yuck!). As the CGT asset was held for more than 12 months only 50 per cent of the capital gain is taxable. As mentioned previously, the 12 months ownership rule commences from the date the deceased bought the property. So if you sell a CGT asset within 12 months of the deceased buying it the entire gain is liable to tax.

Handy tip

If you own property as joint tenants (for instance, husband and wife), in the event of your death, your legal interest in the property will automatically pass to the surviving joint tenant. On the other hand, if you own property as tenants in common, you can nominate the beneficiary who should receive your legal interest in the property in your will.

Exempt assets

Two notable assets that are specifically exempt from the CGT provisions are the deceased's main residence and any cars the deceased owned. With respect to the deceased's main residence, the beneficiary will be deemed to have acquired it on the date of death at its *market value*. The great news here is if the property were to become the beneficiary's main residence it will continue to be exempt from tax. Alternatively, if the property is sold within two years of the deceased's death any capital gain on sale will be exempt from tax. If you sell the property after two years it will no longer be exempt. In the meantime, if you lease the property and then sell it within two years you will still get the full exemption.

Distributing assets: the wisdom of Solomon

Given that certain assets are taxed differently under the CGT provisions, it could become an important issue to consider when distributing assets to your nominated beneficiaries. This is especially the case if you happen to own:

$ investments such as shares, property and collectables that you purchased before 20 September 1985 that have appreciated substantially in value

$ an investment portfolio (for instance, shares and property) you purchased on or after 20 September 1985 that has gone through the roof since you bought them

$ a main residence that's worth millions of dollars

$ collectables such as artwork or a valuable stamp collection

$ a much-sought-after Ferrari

$ a superannuation pension.

It could become a mind-boggling exercise if you have to decide who should get your exempt assets, assets you acquired before 20 September 1985 and assets you acquired on or after 20 September 1985. You may need the wisdom of Solomon to solve this problem as each type of asset will be taxed differently under the CGT provisions. I suppose the most aggrieved will be those beneficiaries who find they've inherited a potential nasty tax bill down the track! But as they say in the classics, beggars can't be choosers.

Sharing your superannuation pension

If you're in receipt of a superannuation pension at the time of your death (for instance, an account-based pension), your pension payments can continue to be paid to your dependants until all your super fund benefits have been diminished. Alternatively, the balance in your super fund account can be paid to your estate. If you still have any superannuation benefits sitting in an accumulation account, they can be paid to your nominated beneficiaries or to your estate. Under Australian tax law the following beneficiaries are dependants for the purposes of receiving your superannuation pension:

$ spouse, de facto spouse, former spouse

$ child less than 18 years of age

$ person financially dependent on deceased at the date of death

$ person in an 'interdependency relationship'.

By the way, if your beneficiary is a dependant child the pension can continue to be paid until the child turns 18 years of age. It will then become a tax-free superannuation lump sum death benefit payment. If your dependant child happens to be permanently disabled the payment can continue to be paid as a pension to that person.

Handy tip

If you want your superannuation pension to be distributed to a specific dependant in the event of your death (for instance, your spouse), make sure you sign a 'binding death benefit nomination form'. If you do this the trustee of your super fund must follow your instructions. This form must be renewed every three years. If you don't do this, there's a risk that the trustee may not follow your instructions to distribute to your nominated dependant. You can get this form from your superannuation fund.

Glossary

account-based pension A superannuation pension where you can vary your pension payments each year and continue to be paid until your funds are diminished. You must receive a prescribed minimum each year which can vary from between 4 per cent and 14 per cent of your account balance.

All Ordinaries index An index used to measure the movements in Australian share prices.

American style A term to indicate the holder of a warrant has the right to buy or sell the underlying shares at any time up to the expiry date.

assessable income Assessable income is ordinary income and statutory income that will be liable to tax.

bank bills A short-term investment with a bank that you purchase at a discount to its face value. When the investment matures you will be paid its face value.

blue chip A company that's well established and trading profitably.

bonds Interest-bearing securities normally issued by governments that offer a fixed rate of interest. When the bond matures the holder will get back the face value (being the amount originally invested). Bonds can be bought and sold on the Australian Securities Exchange.

bridging loan This is a short-term loan that you take out to cover your position while another financial transaction you had entered into is in the course of being completed.

budget A financial plan that will allow you to keep track of all your income and expenses.

business activity statement A statement under the pay as you go tax system that you prepare at the end of each reporting period disclosing certain income that is liable to income tax.

buy contract note An invoice you receive from a stockbroker at the time you purchase shares. It will summarise the details of the transaction and is used to calculate a capital gain or capital loss for taxation purposes.

call option An option that gives the holder the right, but not the obligation, to buy the underlying shares at an agreed price on or before the expiry date. A call option is worth buying in a rising market.

capital gain A gain you make when you sell a CGT asset for a price greater than its cost base. Under Australian income tax law a capital gain is liable to tax.

capital gains tax (CGT) A tax on gains you make on disposal of CGT assets (for instance, shares and real estate) that you acquire on or after the 20 September 1985.

capital loss A loss you incur when you sell a CGT asset for a price below its reduced cost price. Under Australian tax law a capital loss can only be deducted from a capital gain.

capital proceeds Money you receive on sale of an investment asset.

capital protection loans A loan to buy shares where you can protect yourself from incurring a loss if your share portfolio falls in value. These are normally non-recourse loans where the lender rather than the investor suffers any potential loss. You will be charged a high rate of interest.

cash management account A bank account that pays you interest at the end of each month and allows you to make regular deposits and cheque withdrawals.

CGT asset This is an asset (for instance, shares, collectables and real estate) that is liable to income tax under the capital gains tax provisions.

collectables These are assets like antiques, paintings, rare books, stamps, coins and jewellery. Collectables that cost more than $500 fall for consideration under the capital gains tax provisions.

complying superannuation fund A fund that has made an election to be regulated under the *Superannuation Industry (Supervision) Act*. Complying super funds are taxed at the rate of 15 per cent and can pay pensions to their members.

concessional contribution A contribution you make to a complying super fund that qualifies for a tax deduction. These contributions are liable to tax in the super fund.

condition of release A condition you must satisfy before you can access your benefits in a superannuation fund. The most common condition is when you retire.

contract for difference (CFD) A derivative that allows you to speculate in the price movement of underlying securities (such as shares) without actually owning them outright.

cost base Under the capital gains tax provisions, the price and costs you pay for CGT assets like shares, real estate and collectables. It can also include sale costs and other associated costs (for instance, advertising and legal costs) that you may incur.

credit cards Unsecured loans that allow you to access small amounts of cash immediately and/or pay for items you purchase. You will be charged a high rate of interest.

cum dividend This means buying shares that give you the right to receive a dividend that had been declared. The buyer rather than the seller of the shares will become entitled to receive the dividend payment.

debentures Medium- to long-term unsecured interest-bearing securities issued by companies. Debentures pay a fixed rate of interest during the term of the loan.

discount capital gain A capital gain on disposal of CGT assets that were owned for at least 12 months. Only half the capital gain you make on disposal is liable to tax. The other half is exempt.

discretionary trust A trust where the trustee has discretion as to how the trust net income should be distributed to the beneficiaries.

dividend A distribution of company profits to its shareholders.

dividend franking credit A tax offset you receive from a dividend that is franked.

dividend reinvestment plan An agreement with the company that gives you the right to receive additional shares (normally at a discount, and no brokerage is payable) in lieu of a cash dividend payment.

dividend yield The rate of return on your investment in shares.

earnings per share The amount of net profit a company earns expressed on a per-share basis. For example, if a company has issued 10 million shares and earns $1 million net profit, its earnings per share is 10 cents per share.

European style A term to indicate the holder of a warrant has a right but not the obligation to buy or sell the underlying shares on the expiry date.

exercise price The price holders of call options or call warrants must pay if they elect to exercise their right to buy the underlying shares. Also the price holders of put options or put warrants receive if they exercise their right to sell the underlying shares.

ex-dividend These are shares that do not give you the right to receive a dividend. The dividend payment will go to the seller of those shares.

final dividend A dividend that is paid at the end of the financial year.

fixed-interest securities Investments such as term deposits that pay you a fixed rate of interest over the term of the investment.

fixed-rate loan A loan where the rate of interest is fixed for a certain period of time.

franked dividend A dividend that gives you the right to receive a franking tax offset or credit. The offset is applied against the tax payable.

goods and services tax (GST) A 10 per cent goods and services tax on your purchases and sales. Commonly referred to as GST.

holding statement A statement you receive from a company confirming the number of shares you own.

home loans A loan to purchase your main residence. It will have specific features tailored to suit your particular circumstances.

indexed cost base The purchase price of a CGT asset that you acquired prior to 21 September 1999 plus certain costs you incur that have been adjusted for inflation.

industry funds Superannuation funds set up for specific industries. They are generally not-for-profit funds that are open to the general public.

initial repairs Repairs that you make to a newly acquired property. Under Australian tax law these repairs are not tax deductible expenses.

instalment activity statement A statement under the pay as you go tax system that you prepare at the end of each reporting period disclosing certain income that is liable to tax.

interest-only loans A loan where you're only required to repay interest over a certain period of time. The principal is repaid at a later date or when the loan matures.

interim dividend A dividend that is normally paid part way through the financial year.

joint ownership Owning investments jointly (for instance, as husband and wife).

joint tenant A term associated with owning real estate jointly (for instance, as husband and wife). In the event of the death of a joint tenant legal title will automatically pass to the surviving joint tenant.

line of credit loan A loan where you can access finance up to an approved predetermined limit. You will normally offer property as collateral to secure the loan.

listed company A company that is listed on the Australian Securities Exchange.

low doc loans A loan where no documentary evidence is required to verify your capacity to repay. They are normally offered to high-risk investors at a high rate of interest.

main residence A place where you normally reside. It can include up to two hectares of land that surrounds your home. Your main residence is normally exempt from tax under the capital gains tax provisions.

managed funds Mutual or pooled investment funds managed by Australia's leading financial institutions (such as banks and insurance companies) that give investors the opportunity to invest in a wide range of domestic and foreign investment portfolios.

margin loans A financial arrangement where you'll use a combination of your own capital and borrowings to fund a share portfolio. If the value of your shares fall you'll be liable to make good the shortfall (referred to as a margin call).

marginal rate of tax The rate of tax payable on the last taxable income dollar you earn. The rate can vary from between 0 per cent to 45 per cent.

market price The current value of an asset that you can buy or sell on the open market.

Medicare levy A medical levy based on a percentage of your taxable income (currently 1.5 per cent)

negative gearing A term associated with borrowing money to buy wealth creation assets such as shares and real estate. You will be negative gearing when your expenses (particularly interest payments) exceed the income you derive.

net tangible asset The net value of a company expressed on a per-share basis.

non–account based pension Normally lifetime pensions, which means you'll be guaranteed a pension for the rest of your life. Your pension payments can only increase to counter the impact of inflation.

non-concessional contribution A contribution you make to a complying superannuation fund that does not qualify for a tax deduction.

non-deductible holding costs Under the capital gains tax provisions, these are expenses like interest payments, rates and land taxes, repairs and insurance that you incur on non–income producing investments that you acquire on or after 20 August 1991. These outlays can be included in the cost base of a CGT asset.

non-discount capital gain A capital gain on disposal of CGT assets that you had owned for less than 12 months. The entire capital gain is liable to tax.

preserved benefits Superannuation fund benefits that you can access when you reach your preservation age and retire.

personal loans These are normally unsecured loans that you can take out for a specific purpose (for instance, to buy a car or shares).

positive gearing A term associated with borrowing money to buy wealth creation assets such as shares and real estate. You are positive gearing when your investment income (cash inflows) exceeds your investment expenses (cash outflows).

preservation age The age you must reach before you can access your superannuation fund benefits. Depending on when you're born this can very from between 55 and 60 years of age.

price/earnings ratio Shows the relationship of a company's current market price relative to its earnings per share.

principal plus interest loans A loan where you'll pay back both interest and principal at regular intervals (for instance, fortnightly or monthly).

product disclosure statement A legal document that must be prepared when raising finance. It will set out relevant information about the investment products, the benefits and risks and fees you'll be charged.

property trust A managed fund that invests predominantly in major residential and commercial property developments located throughout Australia.

public sector funds Superannuation funds set up specifically for public servants.

put option A form of insurance that gives the holder the right, but not the obligation, to sell the underlying shares at an agreed price on or before the expiry date. A put option is worth buying in a falling market.

put warrant Gives the holder the right, but not the obligation, to sell the underlying shares to the issuer (usually a financial institution) at an agreed price on or before the expiry date.

reduced cost base Similar to the cost base of a CGT asset minus certain expenditure that had been allowed as a tax deduction (for instance, capital works deduction). It is used to calculate a capital loss.

restricted non-preserved Superannuation fund benefits that you can access when you retire or satisfy a condition of release (for instance, you terminate your current employment).

retail funds Superannuation funds set up by Australia's leading financial institutions such as banks and life insurance companies that are open to the general public.

reverse mortgage loans Loans that allow borrowers over a certain age (for instance, 60) who own property to draw down cash. No repayments are necessary until the property is sold. In the event of death any amount outstanding is recouped from the estate.

rights issue The right to buy additional shares direct from the company at a specified price (usually below market price) on a specified future date.

savings accounts A bank account that pays interest on money deposited. The investor can make regular deposits and withdrawals.

self-managed superannuation fund A superannuation fund that you manage yourself.

sell contract note An invoice you receive from a stockbroker at the time you sell your shares. It will summarise the details of the transaction and can be used to calculate a capital gain or capital loss for taxation purposes.

shareholder dividend statement A statement you receive from a company setting out the details of a dividend payment.

sole purpose test A test to check that the dominant reason for setting up a self-managed super fund is to provide benefits to members upon retirement, and provide benefits to dependants in the event of a member's death.

stockbroker A person authorised to buy and sell shares on the Australian Securities Exchange. Stockbrokers charge a brokerage fee for their services.

superannuation fund A fund set up to finance retirement strategies. Money cannot be normally accessed until you reach at least 55 years of age and you retire from the work force. A superannuation fund can pay you a pension.

taxable income The amount of income that is liable to income tax.

tax file number A number issued by the Australian Taxation Office to identify individuals and companies who lodge tax returns.

tax offset A tax credit or rebate that you can use to reduce the amount of tax payable on taxable income derived.

tenants in common A term associated with owning real estate jointly (for instance, as business partners). In the event of death legal title to the property can be transferred to the deceased's beneficiaries.

term deposits A savings account with a bank that pays a fixed rate of interest for a specific period of time. Financial penalties may apply if funds are withdrawn before the maturity date.

transition to retirement pension A superannuation pension that you can purchase when you turn 55 years of age and while still continue working on a full-time or part-time basis. The amount you can withdraw each year must fall between four per cent and 10 per cent of the balance in your superannuation fund account.

underlying shares The shares that you will actually buy or sell.

unfranked dividend A dividend that does not entitle you to receive a franking credit.

unrestricted non-preserved Superannuation fund benefits that you can access immediately.

unsecured notes An unsecured investment normally issued by finance companies that pay a high rate of interest during the term of the loan. The investor has no specific claims over the company's assets.

variable-rate loan A loan where interest rates will vary in line with the prevailing market.

vendor finance loans A loan where the vendor (for instance, property developer) provides the necessary finance to the purchaser to buy a property.

warrant A warrant gives the purchaser the right, but not the obligation, to buy or sell underlying securities (such as shares) within a certain period of time. Warrants are normally issued by major Australian banks and can be traded on the Australian Securities Exchange.

wash sale Selling shares to make a capital loss and gain a tax benefit, then buying the shares back immediately.

will A legal document setting out your final instructions as to who should get your assets and personal belongings in the event of your death.

yield The return you receive on your investment expressed as a percentage.

Index